What happens to us when we think

What happens to us when we think

Transformation and Reality

MICHAEL GELVEN

STATE UNIVERSITY OF NEW YORK PRESS

Published by
STATE UNIVERSITY OF NEW YORK PRESS
ALBANY

© 2003 State University of New York

For information, address
State University of New York Press
90 State Street, Suite 700, Albany, NY 12207

Production, Laurie Searl
Marketing, Anne M. Valentine

Library of Congress Cataloging-in-Publication Data

Gelven, Michael.
   What happens to us when we think : transformation and reality / Michael
Gelven.
      p. cm.
   Includes index.
   ISBN 0-7914-5747-8 (alk. paper)—ISBN 0-7914-5748-6 (pbk. : alk. paper)
      1. Metaphysics—Psychological aspects.   2. Thought and thinking.   3. Change.
   I. Title.

BD111.G45 2003
110—dc21   2002192954

10 9 8 7 6 5 4 3 2 1

to

Sebastian Stark

and

Nathan Birkholz

Contents

ONE

Transformations

1

Down the dark, wet street of the inner city lurked armed gangs, scurrying rats, bumps of drug-lacerated humanity huddled in the soft rain, feral dogs—and in deep peril, his friend.

Don't be afraid.

But I am afraid. I wish I weren't, but I am, so don't tell me not to be! Who wouldn't be? There are damn good reasons to be afraid. This is a killer's street.

Those sound like excellent reasons just to leave.

I know, but I can't. My friend is in trouble; I should go help him. But I'm too scared.

He needs your help whether you're afraid or not.

I know that. Why do you think I'm afraid? If it weren't for him needing me, I wouldn't be afraid at all; I wouldn't even be here; I'd be home. Unafraid, and safe.

But if he needs you, shouldn't you help him?

Aren't you listening? I'm afraid. I'm afraid to stay; I'm afraid to leave. I don't want to be shot and killed; I don't want to go home knowing I left him when he needed me. So I'm afraid either way! Oh, God! I wish I weren't so . . . I don't know: I wish I weren't so scared.

Fear is a natural thing. It's nature's way of ensuring survival. Being afraid may be keeping you alive right now.

Nature's way, huh? That doesn't help any. Even if it weren't natural I'd still be afraid. So would you. So *are* you!

Why do you say I'm afraid?

You're scared, too. I'm afraid of a dangerous street; you're afraid of a word. A mere word. You're afraid to say that word, aren't you? Just now, when I said I wish I weren't so . . . and then broke off—you expected another word didn't you? So go ahead, say it!

What word do you want me to say?

Chicken.

Are you calling me chicken? Or is that what you think I'm afraid to say? It's about courage, isn't it? You're afraid of being shot if you go down that street; you're afraid of being called a coward if you don't.

I don't give a damn about being called a coward. I'm afraid of being one. We're both cowards.

Not entirely. Not if you're still here. But it's transformed now, isn't it? It's not just a natural thing anymore, is it? Maybe fear never is just fear, at least for the thoughtful or the hesitant. You're right about one thing, though: it was wrong to tell you not to be afraid; I should have urged you to take courage. You spotted that; it took a little courage even to spot it.

So here I am shaking like air coming out of a jet, and just because I say "chicken" I get a medal for bravery? Good thinking!

Somehow I don't think you'll be standing here much longer. You see, you've transformed everything now, including yourself, just with that one word, courage.

But I'm still scared.

I know. But now it means something entirely different.

2

It's so easy to get lost in this charming old city. Where are we?

I'm not sure. Do you see that yellow stone building over there, next to the park?

Yes, I see it. What is it?

I don't know.

Then why did you point it out?

Do I have to know what it is to point it out?

Well, Einstein, if we want to get back to the hotel, what good is it to note that building if it's not on this tourist map?

Getting back to the hotel isn't the only thing that matters, you know.

It's not the only thing that matters, I agree; but it is one thing that does. I don't see any use at all to point out a building without knowing what it is or where it is. You don't just look at a building for no reason.

If we were in Agra wouldn't you look at the Taj Mahal, or in London, wouldn't you look at the Tower?

Of course I would. Those are tourist sights. They are monuments.

So you let a tourist map tell you what to see? You can go home and tell everybody you saw the Tower of London. Bragging rights.

We're not in London. If we were, I'd go to see the Tower. And I'd see it because Elizabeth was imprisoned there and all kinds of famous people lost their heads. It's an historically interesting spot.

And that yellow building isn't?

I don't know whether it is or not.

If I told you a famous person was killed there, would you then find it worthy of being looked at?

Sure, why not? It does look like someone important might have died there, come to think of it. Maybe we could ask someone.

I can't believe this. You'd look at that building only if you knew it was historically interesting?

Don't be so superior. What's wrong with history?

Nothing's wrong with history. I love to visit historical places, too. But a sense of history isn't the only reason to look at a building.

Sure. And one of the most important reasons is to use it as a landmark to find our way back to the hotel. I'm hungry. If that yellow building has a restaurant or pub or grill or whatever they call it in this country, I'll take interest in it.

Now, look. You're being deliberately otiose. I ask you, as a favor. Just look at that building.

All right. I'm looking. Now what?

Well . . . isn't it interesting?

What would give it *interest*? History would. Food would. If it's a store, merchandise would. Why is it interesting? How could it possibly *interest* me if I don't know what it *is*?

Good Lord! Why do we always get into these arguments? But, you're right about one thing. I misspoke. Interest does require a context, doesn't it? What happens if you look at that building without any context at all: no history, no use, no utility, not even shelter. If we agree that the building is entirely uninteresting, and yet I still want you to look at it, what would you say?

Probably something about your age and what it's doing to your brain cells. Something along those lines.

For heaven's sake. Look at the architecture.

Architecture! Here I am starving and lost and you talk about architecture?

We had breakfast an hour ago; and we're not lost in any real sense because there are taxicabs and polite people in shops who would tell us where we are. Look at that yellow building, *please*.

But I've never studied architecture. And isn't architecture history? Oh, very well. Let's see . . . It is lovely. Indeed it's beautiful, isn't it? It's rather serene, yet protective in its strength. How did he manage that, I wonder? The architect, I mean. Perhaps it's because those stones are cut in oblong shapes, and he uses them both horizontally and vertically in different places. The eye is led upward by the vertical—see! Yet it doesn't soar, like a cathedral; its breadth gives it a solidity that pleases just because it mutes its power, offering welcome, too. Its elegance, though, suggests it's not just anyone whom it welcomes, only the elite. Perhaps that's what the architect wanted to do: welcome the elite warmly; but with institutional security.

You may be right. Wait a minute. Give me that guide book and map. Why, here it is. Yes, it *is* on the map. It's a famous convent school—

Of course it is. You can *see* it is. You don't need a guide map.

You've changed your tune. I thought you *liked* maps.

I like maps if I want to get somewhere or know where I am. But just looking is different. It was that one word: *architecture*. That transformed everything, didn't it? How silly of you not to have noticed.

I? *I* not noticed? I can't believe this. Which of us didn't notice?

You didn't, you philistine. You kept talking about interest, not noting that interest forfeits the art. You finally got me to look; only now 'look' means something entirely different.

3

Ladies and gentlemen of the jury; you have heard the counselor for the prosecution sum up her case against my client. She is a skilled, indeed artful attorney, and has succeeded in bringing together the various elements of both circumstantial and direct evidence into a coherent scenario. It is her job to prosecute, and one of the reasons she has an enviable reputation for success is her ability to make her version of the story so believable—so rational, if you will—that you, as jurors, will be persuaded that any other account seems artificial or strained. She has done that in this case. Her account is believable. Her account makes sense. But in a court of law, ladies and gentlemen, it is not enough to offer a coherent and sensible account. It is necessary that any alternative story that would acquit my client is so unlikely that you would have to judge it to be unreasonable. The counsel for the prosecution has tried to do this, too. She has tried to show that what you would have to assume in order to acquit my client is simply beyond our normal understanding of what is reasonable.

Ladies and gentlemen, I have been a public defender for many years; and as I'm sure you know, all of us in the public defender's office have very heavy caseloads; sometimes we barely have enough time to read all the files, which include the prosecutor's briefs. I'm not complaining about this—I mention it only to explain that over the years I have found it both helpful and necessary to listen very closely to a prosecutor's summing up. I have won a few cases by attending avidly to these summaries—not only to what they contain, but sometimes, more tellingly, to what they do not contain; or rather, to what they skim over. For I have learned that what is skimmed over is sometimes skimmed because there's a weakness there. When a prosecutor takes a breezy or relaxed attitude toward a facet in the case, glossing or dismissing it lightly, I prick up my ears. Not always, but often enough, this glibness alerts me to increase my suspicion. They, the prosecutors, don't realize that when they trivialize, they're doing my job for me. I'm always grateful when they lighten up. I am grateful today.

Did the counsel for the prosecution, at any time during her summing up, wave anything aside as unimportant? Did she ask you, in your hearing, to hurry past a subtle point, lest the overall thrust of her way of telling the story be missed? If she did this, and I think she did, we must ask why? Let us review what she said, to see if you, the jury, can remember a moment when the pace of her account lightened a bit, when her tone became friendly, whimsical, inviting just a touch of bright contempt, making you feel a little easier in hurrying past a point; hurrying past it, ladies and gentlemen, so that you would not think about it.

Her initial witness was the police officer who first arrived at the scene. He testified that, in a response to a dispatch, he found my client in the back of a warehouse, wiping off a heavy metal bar. The night watchman was lying unconscious on the floor, and the back entrance to the warehouse had been forced open. This officer further testified that the crime lab had found evidence on the bar suggesting it was used to force open the rear door, and positive evidence—blood—proving it had been used to strike a hearty blow—luckily not fatal—at the back of the watchman's skull. Outside, in a large burlap sack were several boxes of rare and very expensive items taken from the warehouse. These are facts that are not is dispute. Nor is it in dispute that a merchant in the shop next to the warehouse had through his window seen my young client come out of the forced exit at the rear, pick up a burlap bag on the landing, and then, after hesitating, put down the bag, and return into the building. The merchant immediately called the police. You have heard the merchant testify to this. You also heard testimony from a certain Scott Wilson, who is my client's coach for the church baseball team and who had become something of a mentor and guide to the young man. You heard this kindly gentleman testify he had received a warning by telephone from an unnamed caller who had informed him that my client might be in trouble at that address. According to his testimony, he arrived just minutes after the merchant called; indeed he arrived at the scene while the policeman was in the act of arresting my client.

Mr. Wilson's testimony is particularly damaging, for he is a reluctant witness, a very reluctant witness, with obvious fondness for the boy. Yet, under the prosecution's careful questioning, he was forced to admit my client was going through what he calls a phase of alienation, and had spoken of wanting to do something remarkable. Further, his testimony completely reinforces that of the arresting officer; Mr. Wilson also saw my client with the iron bar still in his hand, with a cloth wrapped around the bar.

The counsel for the prosecution noted that the crime lab was unable to find any prints at all on the iron bar or on the boxes of the precious merchandise. Since my client was found wiping the bar with a cloth, his guilt seems ineluctable. According to the prosecutor, my client, after forcing open the rear door with the iron bar, used it to knock out the watchman from behind, and after taking the various boxes of expensive items and putting them in the sack, only then, realizing his prints might indict him, in something of a panic, first wiped the boxes in the bag and then returned to the warehouse to wipe off the bar. Since no one else, except, of course, for Mr. Wilson and the arresting officer, was seen in the area, the evidence seems to doom my client.

Finally, you heard the testimony of the detective who interrogated my client at the police station. According to the detective, the defendant, after waiving his right to counsel, admitted he had wiped the iron bar and the cases of stolen merchandise, but denied he had committed either the felonious act of grand larceny or the felonious attack on the watchman. To the felonious charge of obstructing justice by tampering with the evidence, the defendant curiously remains silent. When asked why he wiped the bar and the boxes, he does not answer. He is remarkably taciturn about his motives. He would not even tell me, his own attorney. I was in the dark about his reticence as much as you.

When the counselor for the prosecution came to this point in her summing up, what did she say? She smiled at you, and asked you—and I'm quoting her exactly here— "why wouldn't he explain his motives? Well, would you?"

Ladies and gentlemen of the jury, as I sat here listening to her sum up her formidable case against my client, that question of hers simply did not ring true. Everything else did; she tells a compelling story. Why did she ask, "would you?" One would have expected her to explain that the most obvious reason for keeping silent about his motive for wiping off the bar was that there could *be* only one reason—a reason that would indict him—namely, to erase his fingerprints. But she did not say that. Why didn't she? We might speculate. Is it because she realizes that focusing on the motivation for the single act of wiping the iron bar would raise the question about the one part of her case—one part of *this* case—that is a little puzzling? For here is the problem: the boy must surely know that if he did not break open the door, strike the watchman, and steal the merchandise, he would have no apparent reason to wipe the bar. But if he had no reason to wipe the bar, neither did he have reason to wipe the merchandise. Indeed it is the fact that the merchandise is also wiped clean of all fingerprints that makes us pause. Yes, of course, if he had struck the watchman he would have wiped the bar; but why, at the scene of the crime, when time was precious, would he wipe all of the boxes? Why wipe them *first*? Why not simply run away? This is the line of thought the prosecution does not want you to take, so she directed your attention to the motive for wiping the bar, but not by stating the obvious motive, but by asking if *you* would have done so. You—each of you—realized immediately why you would have wiped the bar; and you then would have assumed the question of motive was settled, and with that motive settled, so would be his guilt. But though the motive for wiping the bar might be explained, the same motive cannot possibly be ascribed to wiping the boxes. The prosecution does not want you to think about that. Rather, she points to his silence, to his reticence, about his motivation, as an indicator of his guilt. "His silence damns him," she said—and again I quote her directly from the transcript. But does it?

Why wipe the boxes? And more important, why remain silent about your motive? All we need is a suggestion; indeed one word will do it. It transforms everything, so that we must read the obvious backward. Perhaps this boy is not a liar as the prosecution says, but every word he says is true. Perhaps he was not taking the merchandise away, but bringing it back. He was not trying to escape, but was allowing himself to be caught if necessary. He did not erase his fingerprints from the bar or the boxes, but the fingerprints of another. He is willing to go to prison so that the other would not have to. But he simply could not, even to protect someone, lie; for he had taken an oath, and to him an oath is sacred. That's the kind of boy he is. The remarkable thing he said to his mentor that he wanted to do was not to steal, but to sacrifice. To ensure this, he did not even want a lawyer, but the judge would not let so young a defendant try his own case, so I, a mere public defender, was appointed. He would not talk to me about that night at all. Above all, even now, he remains silent about the one thing that would be the easiest to explain away. The one word I offer to you that enables us to see why he wiped the bar *and* the boxes, why he must remain silent on his motive and still keep his oath to tell the truth, indeed why he is here at all, is loyalty. Loyalty is the supreme virtue of a noble youth. It is the ground even of his remarkable, if imprudent, sacrifice. His silence is to the counsel for the prosecution an indication of his guilt. But with that one word, *loyalty*, the scenario is transformed from a base story of venal crime to a noble story of great sacrifice. One who is loyal is usually reluctant, ever, to lie under oath. To the prosecution, his silence convicts; but with the suggestion of the word *loyalty* his silence acquits, for now it means something entirely different.

4

What do you think about that theory we heard in the metaphysics seminar today?

There were too many theories in that seminar. I'm tired of theories.

Yes, well—I guess I don't mean just another theory; it's what you might call a metatheory. You scowl?

What a vile phrase. I suppose metatheories are then ranked by meta-metatheories. How silly it all seems.

Why, how saucy you are! Whatever else could metaphysics be except theory—a theory of reality.

Saucy? Perhaps I am a bit saucy. I sometimes feel so outclassed by the others in the seminar. They all seem to thrive on it—as you do. But . . .

Ah, yes. There's always that word *but*. Spelled with one *t*, so as not to fan your sauciness. You're disingenuous, you know. That's the academic word for 'saucy'. You don't feel outclassed, you feel superior. You may be new to our graduate program, but don't play the injured innocent to me. I'm your friend, and know you too well. You think we're just *wrong*.

If sauciness be a species of honesty, then, excluding you, I think everyone in that seminar, especially the professor, is wrong.

In what way, wrong?

They leave out the bump . . . The bump of the real.

What *can* you mean?

They offer up alternative theories as packaged games, marketed by cleverness, to entertain the buyer—in this case, the student. They don't ever seem to ask, seriously, whether any theory is true, much less real; and that's caused in part by their insistence that even those words, *true* and *real*, are already contained and perhaps found only in the plastic-wrapped packages.

That might be an indictment merely of how the professor runs the class. You don't have to treat the theories we read as untrue or as mere alternatives.

That's what I thought at first. But it's deeper than that. Consider what we do, or what we are expected to do. We study theories of reality without studying reality itself. Romeo does not consider theories of beauty when he sees Juliet, his sudden awareness of and slavery to her beauty is a bump. Neither do the hungry consider theories of nutrition when they reach for food. A good practitioner does not consider theories of health, he seeks remedies for those who are sick. By analogy, those who study metaphysics should not study only theories of reality but reality itself.

What is reality itself?

That's the point. I'm not sure. But I am aware of my reality. I don't need a theory to tell me that.

So you think Descartes is right? Begin with a metaphysics of the self.

Descartes begins his metaphysics with a ball of wax. That's his model for what's real: a substance like wax that persists as wax through the changes of its properties. He applies that to his own existence—with disastrous results. He is almost the paradigm of what I mean: he lets his theory explain himself.

But whatever explains us just is, as explanation, theoretical. His theory may be wrong, but it doesn't follow every theory is wrong.

And how do you find out whether a theory is wrong or right? Leave aside internal consistency, which I agree is a necessity. Among consistent theories, don't all explain everything? But they can't all be right, since they contradict.

What about adequacy?

Good. But to judge a theory as adequate you need to have resource to some extratheoretical bump, especially of oneself, to test for adequacy. Look— I'm not denying the need for some sense of internal coherence or theoretical structure; I'm simply saying the word *real* is not captive of any theory *as* theory. Whatever we think about reality outside a system or theoretical account is surely a part of what we mean by metaphysics.

What *is* reality outside a system or theory?

Look. If I imagine a desk right here, I can nevertheless still pass my hand through the space. Were there a real desk, however, in trying to pass my hand through it I would bump into it. Perhaps, though, this example is too materialistic. Suppose I had unwarranted guilt feelings which could be alleviated by the discovery of certain facts: I learn I was not responsible for another's suffering, so the guilt feelings vanish. Contrast that with real guilt: no matter how I may try to deny the censure I cannot escape it: I am guilty and need to own up to it and even atone for it. What I'm trying to say by the word *bump* is that reality *obtrudes*; it has something irresistible in it. I am aware of reality just when it is inescapable, like the avalanche blocking my path.

So, according to your theory, no theory is adequate. Your "ism" is anti-ism-ism. You laugh.

Of course I laugh, because your mockery is both friendly and clever. You're trying to show me I can't escape theoretical limits, but you do so in a playful way, as friends should. But my laughter is real and not a theory of laughter, and we are friends and not mere theorists of friendship.

But if I *think* about laughter and friendship, how can I avoid my concern to make them compatible—and to think of them as compatible is to theorize.

The danger is that your attempt to make friendship—perhaps I should say *being* friends—compatible to being risible might eclipse the reality of laughing and friends. Being a real friend is not the result of theorizing.

But if, in addition to being a real friend, I also want to *think* about it, must I not in *some* sense, theorize?

Perhaps, but I don't think so. Let me show you what I mean. Suppose I discover you have committed a misdemeanor. I am torn between being a friend and being a citizen to report you—especially if someone else might be blamed. The sudden burden, washing over me like a cascade, reveals entirely new—that is, unsuspected—dimensions of what it means to be both friend and citizen. I learn something profound I did not realize before; but such learning is not theoretical. I'm not sure it's empirical, either; indeed I'm not sure what to call it but I cannot deny I have not only learned something new, I have also learned something deep and profound: I am somehow changed.

Of course. But few thinkers or theorists deny that experience can add to our understanding.

Excuse me, but you're missing my point. I do not speak of the experience but of the thought. I am thinking—nontheoretically—directly about what it means to be a friend, what it means to be a citizen. I grant later on I can also speculate theoretically about it, but why would you deny I am thinking about the reality of our being friends when I confront, nontheoretically, such agony?

Perhaps you are thinking. What's your point?

Such direct, nontheoretical thinking about the reality of being friends actually changes me in some way. I keep thinking of that comical word *bump;* which I realize is inadequate. At least I want to say this: such learning is not merely *about* friends, it is part of what it means to be friends. I am not some outsider looking in, I am overwhelmed by the reality of what it means to be a citizen and a friend, and that is not the result of theorizing but of thinking directly about being real.

You used the term "overwhelmed." Is that what you mean: we should include in metaphysics the study of our emotions and feelings?

No—at least, I don't think so. I'm not talking about psychological change *in* me but a metaphysical change *of* me. There may be some emotive states that accompany such change; I suspect awe or astonishment might be among them, and I don't think metaphysicians should blush at the opportunity to learn from such feelings; but on the whole I would say that emotive feelings, not being universal, cannot be central; they certainty are not what I mean when I say I can study being real without first constructing a theoretical account of reality.

Maybe. Plato, after all, says philosophy begins in wonder.

And may continue with it. Yes, *wonder* is probably a better word than *awe, astonishment*, or being *overwhelmed*. It is the metaphysical change though that matters.

So you suggest that such learning is a discovery about being a friend in such a way as to change what being a friend means, so that you as thinker are metamorphized by the "bump" of this realization. In a way you're demanding that what happens to us when we think is an essential part of being a thinker.

I suppose that's what I'm doing. Yes. I want to know what happens to me when I think philosophically about me. Perhaps "metamorphosis" is as good a term as any. To think directly about our being real friends must change us as friends, don't you think?

It may. Although when you insert the term "as" I wonder about the accuracy of the word *metamorphosis*. Perhaps *transformation* is more apt.

So that true metaphysical thinking transforms us as thinkers? That sounds closer to what I'm trying to say.

If so, the notion of metaphysical thinking has itself been transformed, for now it means something entirely different.

5

You're the director of this play, so help me out here.

Ah! Well—of course. What passage troubles you?

It's not any one passage. It's Portia herself; or maybe it's the whole play. You see, at first I thought: here's a girl—Shakespeare calls her that—who cleverly outwits the court of Venice to save Antonio's life; gives a whale of a speech about the quality of mercy; plays a fairly dirty trick with the rings on her incompetent husband; and returns to her home a triumph. So I thought that was the key to her character: she's smarter and spiritually stronger than any of the men, and to understand her is to recognize her superiority, and how she manipulates the male-dominated system without sacrificing her femininity. Her only mistake was falling in love with that sappy, useless brat, Bassanio.

Ah! Well, there's some truth in that, of course; but it's a mite . . . political. You say that was your first view. What happened then?

The same thing that always happens when I perform Shakespeare. She becomes a lot more complicated. I don't mind that; a great play needs rich characters. But Portia is not just complicated, she's a . . . I don't know—an enigma. And unless I figure her out, I won't be able to play her.

Ah, well! Maybe it's the other way around. Only by playing her can you figure her out.

That's why we have rehearsals. But how am I to read her lines?

Ah! Her lines? They're fairly straightforward, I should have thought. It seems to me you did quite well in this rehearsal.

"Quite well" is not quite well enough as you know quite well. My delivery was only "quite well" because I have not yet caught the essence of her character.

Perhaps her character develops; she may not be the same Portia at the end as at the beginning.

It would be a dull play if she didn't develop. I sense that, you know. She learns. Maybe that's the point: her learning. There's a scene that suggests this: right after Bassanio chooses the correct casket, she tells him she would be trebled twenty times herself for his sake. But then she adds:

> . . . But the full sum of me
> Is sum of nothing, which, to term in gross,
> Is an unlessoned girl, unschooled, unpractis'd:

Happy in this, she is not yet so old
But she may learn; and happier than this,
She is not bred so dull but she can learn;
Happiest of all is, that her gentle spirit
Commits itself to yours to be directed . . .

Ah! I knew I had chosen the right woman to play Portia. Instinctively you have selected a crucial passage. Her learning, and not her triumph in the court, gives the play a theme worthy of such a splendid character as Portia. But, please, go on. What troubles you about those lines you read so well?

But did I read them *right*? That's the point. Is she serious? What could she learn from *him*? She doesn't need to be trebled twenty times herself to be already sixty times smarter and nobler than that giddy, greedy, green grasshopper of a boy. Is she simply blinded by love, so that she *thinks* he's smarter than she? Or is it a metaphor: her loving is like an education? Or is she ironic: she really means she will teach him. Or is she suggesting that love is the true educator, not Bassanio. But mostly I want to know what she means by the various educational terms, school'd, lesson'd, learn'd. In what way is she to learn? And *what* does she learn?

Ah, well. I know you share the maxim that the text is always the ultimate source. Let's see . . . Can you give me a passage in which she clearly learns something, and even says so?

A passage where she learns? You don't mean her learning how to defeat Shylock? No, I didn't think so. I'm not sure I can. Though, maybe . . . there is one passage that might serve. It's my favorite in the whole play. She and Nerissa are walking back home, at night, and she spots a candle burning in her house, and says: "So shines a good deed in a naughty world."

Ah, yes. Go on. I'll take Nerissa's line: "When the moon shone we did not see the candle."

So doth the greater glory dim the less:
A substitute shines brightly as a king
Until a king be by; and then his state
Empties itself, as doth an inland brook
Into the main of waters. Music! Hark!

It is your music, madam, of the house.

Nothing is good, I see, without respect;
Methinks it sounds much sweeter than by day.

Silence bestows that virtue on it, madam.

The crow doth sing as sweetly as the lark
When neither is attended; and I think
The nightingale, if she sing by day
No better a musician than the wren.
How many things by season season'd are
To their right praise and true perfection!

Ah, I can see why that might be your favorite.

It's magical! It's like a childhood fantasy; so lovely, so serene and charm-ing, you just don't want it to stop. The two girls have walked a long way, and are tired, but as they near their home, you can almost feel their fatigue drop off of them; their soft, gentle language is a balm to the soul. It tells us something about them we didn't realize before; but the enchantment of that scene also contrasts vividly with the harsh calculation of mercantile Venice and the metallic cleverness of the court. Without that scene it would be less a comedy. It doesn't make us laugh; but it makes us feel wonderful. It's full of grace and warmth.

Ah, indeed. You see that: comedy is about fools being foolish, usually as lovers, but the judgment is warm and gracious; its truth is gentle learning.

Somehow I feel this passage shows us about that gentle learning, but I can't quite fit it in. The imagery itself seems to shift. At first, the point seems fairly banal: we note the candle only because it's dark; we note the substitute only because the king is absent. It would seem, especially in the comparison with the king, that the lesser is noted only when the greater is away: but the king is truly greater than the substitute. Is she suggesting Bassanio is like the substitute? He's not so bad if you don't compare him to anyone else? This seems to be the dubious wisdom that we should be thankful for small favors—one that doesn't seem fitting for Portia. But then she suggests the crow and wren *really* sing as sweetly as the nightingale if they are not "attended." Does she mean the virtues are merely in the eye of the onlooker, so that as long as she sees Bassanio as worthy, then he *is* worthy? That's a bit of relativism that might work for Cupid, but not for virtue; Portia is made of sterner stuff than that. Then, though, she seems to make the strongest claim of all; it is the season that brings us to our perfection. Does this mean her boyish husband might grow up to be a worthy mate? Or is this magical moment *her* season? In returning to Belmont, after her conquests of Shylock by means of legal cleverness and Bassanio by means of the trickery with the rings, has she come to her perfection? If this last is correct, it doesn't seem to mesh with the candle's being appreciated only in darkness, or the music only in silence. I'm not even sure whether she is triumphant or humbled; and whichever it is surely would alter how I say the lines.

Ah! Well. You certainly are right that the imagery develops. She not only uses metaphors, she actually spells out their meaning by two differing principles. First she says "nothing is good without respect" meaning 'comparison'; but then she says "things are seasoned by their season." Both of these adages or principles, if you will, are educational. She has learned to judge things by "respect"; she has learned that everything has its season; and it is by that season or ripeness that the thing should be judged.

But translate that for me. What or who has reached its season? Herself? Bassanio? And what is that perspective, that "respect," that enables her to judge things aright?

Ah. Well, you know I'm not sure it is any one thing or person. Perhaps, indeed, Shakespeare means us to understand that the play itself has reached its season.

Ah! Good heavens, I'm beginning to sound like you: starting every sentence with "ah." Oh, well. Yes. That is . . . wait. I'm more confused than ever.

Ah. Oh, dear. Sorry. Forget the "ah." Do you remember the very first line of this play?

Why . . . yes. Antonio says: "In sooth, I know not why I am so sad." What about it?

Why is he sad? And why doesn't he know?

I'm playing Portia, not Antonio.

But the play itself is named *The Merchant of Venice.*

Isn't that Shylock?

No. Shylock is not a merchant; he's a moneylender. Antonio is the merchant.

So the play's about him? How?

In the last act, after all the triumphs, what does Portia do to Antonio?

Do to him? I don't—oh, yes. She welcomes him into her house. Isn't that simply common civility? Wait! I think I'm catching your drift. It's important, somehow, that Portia welcomes Antonio.

It takes something, doesn't it, to welcome your rival into your house?

Her *rival?* Are you saying Antonio and Bassanio were lovers?

There's nothing in the text to suggest that. But there is a great deal in the text to suggest Antonio loves Bassanio.

Aha! So he's sad just because his love is unrequited; and perhaps he does not want to admit to himself he is in love with him, which is why he says he does not know why he's sad. Only a lover would lavish such largesse on that greedy puppy to a degree that is almost embarrassing. He even signs that dire and dreadful bond just so the boy can woo Portia. Ha, again! Bassanio, on his wedding night, leaves Portia untaken and intact, just to be with Antonio. What can she do that would ever equal the sacrifice that Antonio has given him? Bassanio feels both guilt and fondness—are you sure they're not lovers?—and so he leaves *her* for *him*! Were Antonio to die, her boyish husband would feel forever indebted to his ghost.

That's part of it. You're a little harsh on Bassanio, I think. After all, he does love Portia, and in some ways he loves Antonio. I think you are harsh on him because, in playing Portia, you sense he is perhaps unworthy of you. But tell me what it takes for you, Portia, to greet Antonio, whose life she has saved but who is still her rival, into her house?

What it takes? Courage? Sacrifice? A deeper cunning? I'm not sure, though I feel I *should* be sure.

Let me remind you of something. After Shylock is out-Shylocked by Portia in the court, who is it that urges Bassanio to give the young legal clerk—Portia in disguise—his ring of troth?

Antonio, of course. That's symbolic of the whole play, isn't it? In any contest between the two people he loves, Bassanio is always guided by his friend the merchant, not his young bride. But then, how *could* she welcome Antonio to her home?

Well, you've just shown me how. You tell me. Why does she welcome him?

Because of her love for Bassanio, I assume.

Ah, Perhaps. But think further. She out-Antonio's Antonio, too. Antonio sacrifices both his wealth and his life so Bassanio can marry Portia. Portia also gives her wealth to him, and even welcomes her rival for him. But, it is not a begrudging welcome. No, indeed. The audience doesn't feel that at all. She truly welcomes him because she is transformed.

Yes, but why? How is she transformed?

Take it from Antonio's perspective for a moment. Consider *his* learning. At Belmont he suddenly discovers his savior is *his* rival. He is truly noble in court as he offers his life, telling Bassanio not to grieve at his death, and urging him to be happy with Portia. He means that, and Portia sees he means it. He now discovers it was Portia who saved *his* life. Yet, this discovery cuts both ways: although now he must admit he owes her his life, he also realizes *she* now knows how deeply and maybe darkly he loves her husband. Within seconds of learning this, he is welcomed into her house.

Wow. He must have been overwhelmed with a conflict of emotions. Perhaps he senses that only Portia grasps how he loves Bassanio; but at the same time, he realizes how deep *her* love for Bassanio is, too. But why tell me how to perform Antonio? I'm Portia, remember?

Ah, yes. But you see, those two are mirrors of each other in a way—and not merely because they both love the same boy. They are the two noblest characters: they may be the only ones who understand each other. They are kindred in their nobility of spirit. One suggestion might be this: the play opens with Antonio's confession of his saddness and his ignorance of its base. Perhaps only at the very end does he truly realize *why* he was so sad, and why he was ignorant. He is now no longer ignorant. Oddly, he, Antonio, is worthy of her, Portia.

I see. So that's why you wanted me to think about Antonio: he mirrors her.

Yes, in part. Let me ask you to take another perspective. What does Bassanio learn, at the end, however dimly?

"Dimly" says it all. Unless he's totally dim—which I don't think is the case—he learns clearly that she, Portia—me!—will forever be the true lord of Belmont. She may say he is the lord, but we all know she is going to continue to be the head of that household.

And how does that make him feel?

I never gave his feeling a thought. But you want me to. That's odd. I'd say: though he may feel a twinge at this slight on his manhood, quite frankly I don't think he cares that much. I hate to say it, but I think he's proud of her.

I'd say you're absolutely right. And now: how does she feel about him?

You're good at this, you know. That's an interesting question. Somehow I feel a parallel: she knows he's lightweight, and perhaps there is a twinge of regret for having a lump of Jell-O for a husband, but quite honestly I don't think she's going to let that resentment get in the way. She still loves him. She put him through a tough test with the ring, and he failed. But she is perhaps surprised that, though she is disappointed by his weakness, her love has not diminished. Indeed, it may even have increased. That's the ultimate triumph, isn't it? She learns, perhaps to her own surprise, that like the candle in the darkness or the music in the silence, her love is not decreased but increased by her discoveries. Her love is like a good deed shining in a naughty world. Even more, their love is like the real king; the substitute of the king is merely the external manifestation of it. That's what true learning is, isn't it? Knowing the real from the appearance. That line is the pivot of the whole passage, and I think I missed it.

So she learns not from Bassanio exactly, but from her loving Bassanio. And by the mirroring of herself *as* lover in Antonio.

Yes, I think you're right. We spoke of Antonio and Portia mirroring each other; but your favorite passage is not only about mirroring, but about appearance and reality. Bassanio may be weak, but her love is real, and from that reality she learns the truth. The pivotal line is, as you say, the one about a good deed shining in a naughty world. Her discovery of her own joy in loving truly is like the good deed. Here's the point. It doesn't matter if the vast world is naughty: the single good deed *still* shines; indeed it outshines the whole world.

She is *happy* to learn that truth. Portia learns the truth about Bassanio, but in doing so, she learns the greater truth about herself by transforming into a *real* wife, loving truly, regardless of the boy's flaws. Her *love* of Bassanio and not Bassanio is her true teacher. She is transformed by this wisdom, so that Portia becomes—hah!—Portia becomes truly Portia. She trebles herself twenty times. Ha! I know how to play her, now. When she and Nerissa approach Belmont, she is gently *surprised* by her own *joy*! Yes! What she learns is truth; what leads her to this learning is her real love of Bassanio. In her realization of this truth, she is transformed, she has reached her season and is elated by her transformation; the *taste*, if you will, of that truth, is the seasoning, as salt seasons, in her welcome of Antonio. It's still about learning, but now learning, and even truth itself, mean something entirely different.

TWO

Wonder

Wonder—is not precisely knowing
And not precisely knowing not—
A beautiful but bleak condition
He has not lived who has not felt—

Suspense—is his maturer Sister—
Whether Adult delight is Pain
Or of itself a new misgiving—
This is the Gnat that mangles Men—

—Emily Dickinson

It may be the darker side of our reflections; but even so, it cannot be dismissed without excising too much that is ours, too much of truth. Indeed to dismiss wonder entirely strikes us as shallow, as if we were to purchase a peaceful insouciance at a dreadful cost, as Agamemnon sacrificed his daughter Iphegenia for favorable winds, ensuring dreadful consequences. For good or ill, it seems a part of our nature, like growing old regardless of our preference not to. Whether its origin is in our folly or our wisdom, or in both—akin to our being of two parents—it perplexes us, disturbs us, even as it thrills us. The profound Emily of Amherst penetrates its elusive duality: it may be the gnat that mangles us, but we have not lived unless we have been transformed by it. On this loftier level, wonder cannot be waved aside as a passing fancy or a moment of sentiment; it certainly is not a childlike fascination with new things blossoming all around us—that's why she calls it an adult delight. A child's fascination does not mangle men. That we as adults wonder at all is itself wonderful; yet since we wonder in part because truth matters, to wonder is also earnest. Socrates, in Plato's *Theaetetus*, assures us philosophy begins there; perhaps it never can surpass this beginning. Not all wonder is worthy; we can wonder about many things that are not worth it; in the vernacular, 'wonder' becomes a banal substitute for curiosity. Lovers wonder at the curious bondage that brings them curious joy, and mystics wonder at their private disclosures even as they wonder why the rest of us are so unmoved. The contrite wonder at their egregious errors, the reverent wonder at the largesse of the infinite. Yet, almost as if by a curious default, the paradigm of this dubious reflection has, in our western tradition anyway, usually been recognized as the philosopher. The nature or origin of the philosopher's wonder is spotted in the first line of Dickinson's poem: we know, yet we are ignorant—and this awareness of our veridic duality transforms us in a bleak but beautiful way. Being between knowing and not knowing also suspends us, making suspense the maturer sister of wonder, if the poet is right.

This suspension is of a special kind. There is neither wonder nor suspense in not knowing my bank balance while knowing it's raining. The suspense inherent in wonder is between our knowledge and ignorance of the same thing; indeed the suspense that is a sister to wonder consists in knowing intimately what deeply matters in a way that seems incompatible with being ignorant, as if not knowing is surprisingly what I most profoundly but confusedly know. How could I possibly *not* know who I am? Where in the vastness of the universe do I belong? What do I learn about myself by realizing I do not know myself or where I am? In asking these questions I, as thinker, am transformed in my thinking; yet this transformation is not a matter of mere shift in how I think, but in my reality as thinker. I am entirely altered by this realization of myself. What is the nature of this philosophical transformation?

Perhaps we simply cannot help it. Thrown into a messy world we soon discover our own reality is as murky as the rest, and since as thinkers we seek coherence, we are bound to seek it in ourselves where it is most elusive; there is no surcease of our longing merely because we never find what we seek. Perhaps. This suggestion however seems to account for our self-wonder merely as a knottier problem to be solved by greater skills at unraveling. Somehow the phenomenon reflected in Dickinson's poem strikes us as disanalogous to confronting other knotty problems we must solve as sojourners on the estranging earth or wanderers in the opening bowl of space. It is disanalogous to these other problems in part because it is not only the solution that we seek but the meaning behind our wondering.

And yet, it is perhaps misleading to rarify the phenomenon, for it seems to speak not only of the few, but of all. The bleak but beautiful condition is not akin to a rare disease; for if it were we could quarantine the hale majority and dismiss it as an aberration, a misfiring of nature, or a stumble by the gods.

That, too, is part of its anguish: it is at once rare and common, fiercely lonely and warmly shared. Only a tiny few can or even want to delve into the prodigious tomes of Kant or Heidegger, or puzzle with the enigmatic Zeno; yet even the sweepers, builders, miners, and taxi drivers are not only wondered about, but wonder, too—at times profoundly. In this duality, too, we are suspended, between a species of thoughtless banality and lofty discovery. Perhaps it is this singular aspect of being both elitist and egalitarian that wonder reveals itself as linking two ways or modes, the one perhaps a transformation of the other. We cannot ever escape entirely our banality—perhaps it is even salvatory we cannot—but in some sense we must, if wonder is to happen at all—transform, without entirely shedding, its origins. Here the leit-motif, the pivot-word, the present suggestion of what constitutes the key to metaphysical reflection or wonder, intrudes; perhaps it should be said to usurp, or even assail, as in military depredation. What is transformation? Should it be in quotes: what is "transformation"? To suggest that wonder is also a species of transformation itself transforms what might possibly be meant by metaphysics, conceived in its broadest sense, or philosophical inquiry. But what is transformed? Our thinking? Reality itself? The world? Or just the word? Surely it would seem that if we are to speak of the common or the banal as being transformed into the lofty or profound, we must mean at least that there is an ordinary, easily available way of looking at the world and ourselves, which is then replaced by another way of looking at the same things; and this "other way" is here suggested as being somehow better, truer, more profound, or at least more exotic. It is also true that, on occasion, a single word may do it. This does not mean that language has magical powers akin to Merlin mumbling the right syllables to change the prince to a frog; rather the right word, often in a situation that surprises, opens up a way of thinking that reveals the truth unavailable in any other way. The single words *courage, architecture,* and *loyalty* in the first three dialogic sketches in the previous chapter, wreak a transformation precisely because the words are ordinary words, that in the contexts, enables a shift in thinking allowing a fundamental, existential truth to be discovered—a discovery that surprises all the more because the words are ordinary.

New questions now pour out in a frenzy, like beans spilling out of a poked bag, tattooing the floor in a hiss. Quick! they say: tell us what you mean by transforming so we will know how to judge this new suggestion. Impatience has always thwarted learning; ideas must be savored, like good wines, for the flavors are elusive, haunting, teasing. Dickinson reminds us that what tangles men is a gnat; it is a seeming tiny thing, a mere speck, a brief annoyance, ridded by the wave of the hand. That such a minuscule thing as wonder, no bigger than a gnat, should trip us up, fell the mighty, is itself a puzzle—perhaps even a wonder. Being of such diminutive size, perhaps it should be allowed to grow. Why? Do we *want* to be tangled? Or do we want to study the gnat so as to avoid its peril? Transformation itself may be a gnat that snares a lumbering titan into stumbling, who, when he smacks the ground the whole surrounding earth trembles and is itself transformed. Perhaps the topics of philosophical speculation are the titans tangled or even felled by the minuscule gnat of wonder. These giants are brought down suddenly and heavily to our earth; like felled trees, their upper reaches are now made available to us and our axes. Yet our own nature is one of these giant redwoods that seem to dwarf the whole forest: would we even want to bring these wondrous sentinels of high reaching down to our level? It seems a mean, pinched, envious, and petty thing to do, like caging eagles or deconstructing a mighty artwork to market a theory—both are but species of spite. A gnat is pestiferous and irksome; can it truly be a metaphor of wonder? Is transformation a leveling—bring all things down to the lowest grade of digestibility, mashing the great chef's cuisine down to the pablum of baby food so all can eat it but none can taste it?

Thales tells us the world is made of water. We rightly praise him for the start of something impressive and important in the history of our thinking. Yet, there is something gnatlike about it, too. It transforms all things to one thing. The gods and the mountains are really the same thing as the pebble or the itch of a mosquito bite; from the perspective of fundamental unity there is no difference between the king and the brat, the candy and its wrapper. The gnat is transformed into Parmenides, all is really the same One.

Transformation need not always debase. The warning, though is real: there is a danger in the word; to transform is not to reduce. It was Plato who saw the flaw: the unity of the essential and the real does not unrank, but ranks. It is only because one state is more just than another that I can grasp the essence of justice; the reduction of the many to the one is transformed into dialectical ranking and hence a metaphysics of participation; kings are better than their substitutes, but both exist; the sun is brighter than the lamp. It is the ranking that matters, not the matter that ranks. We speak of Plato's forms, and form is the etymological center to transformation. Ordinary things are transformed by extraordinary thinking, called dialectic; and an extraordinary passion, called love, transforms itself into the love of the truth, not of the mere stuff; and it is truth that alone grounds our explanations of things, not only in their sameness but in the difference. We ourselves are transformed by the passion and the way of thinking—transformed into philosophers. The truth is loved, not the fundamental elements, like water, nor even the theoretical accounts themselves, but rather what enables us to render such accounts, and step back from them, even, and judge them, criticize them, refine them. This is transformation on an Everest: the highest of all. We are transformed by this curious ability to rank, to love the truth, not the mere topic, or what the truth is about.

To demand, at this stage, the precise or even stipulative definition of transformation is therefore revealed as retrograde to what we want to do: we want to wonder about wonder for a moment, grasping vaguely that perhaps in some sense to wonder in this way is to transform or to be transformed or to learn about transformation. We shift from the topics of metaphysical inquiry to the process or occurrence of doing it; perhaps even to ask what it means to do it. Doing what? Doing metaphysics? Is it something that can be *done?* Passionately done?

Haste may again prove our undoing. The literal etymology is less passionate: *philos* means friend, not erotic lover, *sophia* means wisdom, not truth: philosophers are simply the friends of wisdom, a much gentler, less daunting group. It is Plato's Socrates who cheats a little on his inference: he claims philosophers love the truth. This might be called open cheating—cheating we don't mind since it is so overt, and since so much greater insight is gained even if it is not inferentially valid. We let Shakespeare cheat like this in his comedies, with Prosperos and Pucks doing mischief with magic; we don't mind accepting the wizardry of the flower making Lysander love Helena rather than Hermia; it's part of the game of drama. But the analogy disturbs, too: if philosophers care about truth, and not mere emotion and certainly not magic, is not this license far too licentious? Perhaps it is; yet it seems a very expensive price to pay for mere correctness and logical hegemony: the critical is essential for thought—all ideas must be challenged—but the rules of inference cannot of themselves produce anything, and the mere negative critique of another's thinking avoids the original task. Wonder is not a calculus or a set of algorithms, nor is it the application of rules. To what are the rules applied? We know too much about our ignorance to be dazzled by logic. We know too much about our weaknesses to be led solely by the romantic lure of a wonder that is mere excitement. The same Socrates who finds eros necessary for his inquiry also calls himself a gadfly as well as a lover. He challenges the unexamined, and we recognize this as an essential part of who the philosopher is. Is Dickinson's gnat a rewrite of gadfly? Must we be tangled, and perhaps even felled, by gnat or gadfly, if wonder is to reach its full season?

We begin not at the beginning but in the middle. The five dialogic sketches in the prior chapter assume as much as they provide. It does not chafe too harshly to suggest that fear can be transformed into courage, or that seeing can be transformed by art into looking. What do we mean by tranformation in these two particular phenomena? We know what it means to be afraid; we also know that we fear. The child sees the dog, feels threatened, and runs away; there is no shame in this, only relief. This suggests fear is a natural instinct designed to protect us from danger; we might even suggest that the evolutionary development naturally rids itself of species that lack fear, for such fearless species are too vulnerable to predation. Even on this natural or evolutionary level, however, we recognize, even by instinct, that there may be times in which attack is a more successful tactic than retreat. We bark back or yell at the dog, and the dog runs away. We may be just as afraid when we attack as when we run, but a species that includes both offense and defense may be more adaptable and hence more likely to survive than a species guarded only by defense. Is courage simply this: the natural instinct of fearing seen from the offensive and not the defensive tactic to rid ourselves of the pain that comes from fear? Perhaps. When we add to this the social instincts that bring us together, we can even suggest it is natural—i.e., evolutionary—to train the young to risk and endure, teaching them when to attack and when to run, sensing that a clan or group that develops such warrior traits is more successful and adaptable than a group that does not train its warriors. Even a seemingly natural account like this—which must yet prove insufficient—can be seen as transformational: each of these evolutionary steps is a transformation to a higher level of personal and societal existence. On this level of explanation, courage as transformed fear is analogous to the butterfly as transformed caterpillar.

In the first sketch, however, it is not simply the young man's fear of being shot coupled to the fear of his self-reproach; it is the internal struggle within himself, externalized dialogically, that enables courage to *appear*, as it were; making it available for us to think about it. This agonizing belongs to the phenomenon as phenomenon—that is, unless the agonizing were there, the two ways of fearing would not mean anything, unless, through agony, it appears—as phenomena must appear to be phenomena—we could not think about its truth. The struggle, opened up by the concrete dialogue, transforms us who read or hear the talk as truly as it transforms the boy from one who simply has two fears to one for whom cowardice and courage are now made possible and hence meaningful. It is not the fearing that explains the courage, it is rather the courage that explains the fear; but now the courage must be seen in terms of the agonizing and not merely the performance of the right kind of fearing. This would mean that were the boy to go to his friend's assistance without the agonizing, he would not be truly courageous, though he still might be brave, and admired for it. If the agonizing is necessary for courage, then we seem to have slipped, almost unawares, into a different way of thinking altogether.

When the frightened boy articulates his torment openly he may discover that the fear that threatens in the street is external, the fear that keeps him where he is internal. When he considers the street, he worries about what will happen *to* him; when he considers going home, he considers what he himself will *become* as a result of his own action. Once the term "courage" is broached, the way he thinks about his own torment is recast: there are no longer merely two possible ways to behave; now one must be seen as worthier than the other. Yet, it is more than that. What he becomes is truer, and hence more real, than what he does. This is not yet moral calculus: it may still be foolish and hence immoral to go down that street: the danger may be so great, and his ability to help his friend may be so paltry, that to opt for the former may be simply reckless. The actual selection here is not the determiner of courage, but the manner of thinking is; so too is the degree to which this thinking changes *him*. The question shifts from Which is the more frightening action? to What am I becoming? This agony—that he may become disgusting in his own eyes—transforms him simply by his realization that who he is and who he becomes matters. Confronting himself, rather than the options, changes him in a profound way: he may never be quite the same. The realization that his own confronting changes him is an existential transformation that far exceeds the mere calculus of a moral dilemma. This transformation is of thinking: he is transformed because his thinking is transformed. Because of this, the reader, too, may be transformed.

To speak of the boy as transformed is not merely to note that he is changed. Existential transformation has a status, just as wonder itself does; though it is difficult to isolate. One might use the term trivially, suggesting that his lunch transforms him from hungry to sated, or that an item in the newspaper transforms him from topically ignorant to topically wise. Though such uses may be sanctioned by dictionaries, it should be obvious that this ubiquity in the vernacular emasculates the philosophical meaning. To suggest his confrontation with fear transforms him entails a certain sense of profundity and long-lasting alteration: he is not merely changed but fundamentally changed. The adverb *fundamentally* now becomes the key; but it unlocks nothing if it serves as a mere replacement, providing circularity: existential transformation requires fundamental change; but we characterize fundamental change as existential transformation. These reflections are not that glib; the term "fundamental" suggests the essential, that which explains rather than is explained; a fundamental principle is one that is not derivable from or reducible to, other principles; it is also a principle that must be assumed or presupposed if a certain way of thinking is to occur at all. When applied to the change that alters the frightened boy, it means that what he learns about himself is ineluctable, inescapable, and illuminating. The agonizing in itself does not mean that he will do the correct and courageous act, nor does it mean he will never again have to face himself in this way, nor does it suggest that the agonizing guarantees his being courageous, though it seems to enable it.

There is something paradoxical in the realization that the familiar can surprise us, and with this surprise to enduce wonder. A key to this may be the already noted distinction between fearing external threats and internal diminution. Although both fearing and courage are familiar notions, when they are thought about in terms of what we ourselves are and might become, the issue becomes fundamental or metaphysical just because we are fundamentally real, suggesting that it is fundamentality itself that surprises, or perhaps does violence to, the essence of the unsurprising: banality. The nature of this violence will be considered shorty. We ourselves are real, but ordinary thinking curiously distracts us from this reality; to be jolted from this distraction is to surprise, even though what surprises us is what is closest to us, our own being real. Courage surprises us because it reveals our reality that had been hidden by nonfundamental thinking. Even so, surprise seems almost by necessity to be brief and sudden, which is why wonder, which can be sustained, is the truer phenomenon.

It may be helpful now briefly to consider the second sketch. In one sense, the analogy is much easier. Art allows us to transform ordinary seeing into what might be called extraordinary looking, by which phrase is meant: looking in such a way as to glean an understanding of essence, or what a thing means. If the analogy holds, we recognize that the transformation from seeing to looking is accomplished by a suspension of context—harking back to the poet's suggestion that the maturer sister of wonder is suspense; only now suspense does not mean the status of being in between two extremes, such as ignorance and knowledge, but rather putting aside or delaying, as we suspend judgment. If we suspend or put aside context or interest, we are left solely with an appreciation of our looking at it, an appreciation that is made available only by first letting our ordinary perception fall away. There are many ways we note this; we speak, for example of "aesthetic distance" removing us from common concern, or of Wordsworth's "emotion recollected in tranquility" or our "suspension of disbelief." These phrases are readily available for those who reflect on the curious power of art to move us without prompting us to practical action. Yet it is not only in the field of literary criticism where we find the necessity to put the ordinary aside. Philosophers as diverse as Plato, Kant, Schopenhauer, Nietzsche, and Heidegger broaden this power of shelving the ordinary to achieve the broadest applications in philosophical truth seeking. Plato, in the fifth book of the *Republic*, urges us to see not the merely beautiful thing, but beauty itself, rejecting one who does not do this as being like someone asleep; Kant shows us the dialectical necessity of distinguishing phenomena, in which the rules of the understanding determine their occurrence, from noumena, which can only be reasoned about in a formal and regulative way; Schopenhauer distinguishes ordinary thinking, as following the principle of sufficient reason, from extraordinary thinking, which abandons that principle and focuses directly on essences; Nietzsche distinguishes the last man, who ranks success and contentment as the highest achievements, from the superman, who alone, by developing contempt for this contentment, can grasp the meaning of existence; Heidegger's distinction between inauthentic and authentic existence makes his entire existential analysis possible; one must flee from the eclipse of self in everydayness to true self-discovery in guilt and knowing of our finitude in death.

What is fascinating about these otherwise radically different thinkers is that each depicts certain concrete experiences as providing an epiphany of sorts that requires violence to escape the shackles of common thinking. For Plato it is the fearsome madness of erotic love; for Schopenhauer it is artistic genius; for Nietzsche it is disgust with oneself; for Heidegger it is conscience and guilt. For Kant, the experience that transforms is ironically the act of thinking metaphysically itself, which transforms us by the huge violence done to our own reasoning by the antinomies. For each of these thinkers, it is not only necessary to put aside limited or common ways of thinking; such putting aside necessitates a specifically violent act, made necessary because the hegemony of the ordinary is so remarkably strong in itself. The philosopher who seems closest to the transformation in the second sketch is Schopenhauer, who argues that artistic genius alone is capable of providing the violence necessary to suspend the principle of sufficient reason. The two tourists in the sketch are in a playful, vacational mood, far removed from the dire seriousness of the first sketch; indeed one might almost sense a comedic touch, as they gently chide and insult each other as only friends can do. Yet, their transformation from seeing to looking is clearly enabled by suspending the power of context and interest. The light, comic tone of the second sketch may not suggest any violence at all; but to do what they did—to extirpate the ordinary—is revealed as an achievement of no small matter. If it is the art of architecture that alone provides the transformation from merely seeing the building to the sheer wonder at it, the violence is there already. We may be pleasantly delighted at the performance of a romantic comedy such as *A Midsummer Night's Dream*, but that does not render erotic love any less violent; it is rather that the violence is rendered acceptable by the comedic art. Art itself must be violent if it is to be understood as the violation of the principle of sufficient reason.

The remark about violence in the thinking of the five philosophers mentioned should not distract the central focus. The point is that we can understand wonder as a transformation that suspends or puts aside ordinary thinking—how could wonder be ordinary? It is Schopenhauer who makes it explicit *what* is put aside—the principle of sufficient reason. For him, the putting aside requires the special violence known as artistic genius. If philosophy is conceived as wonder—and not merely originating in wonder—it, too, is a transformational act that violently puts aside or suspends the common or usual way of thinking. The danger is not that we shall render this transformation as overly exotic; rather it is entirely otherwise: the danger is we will not render it sufficiently exotic. That is why we must focus on wonder; for all wonder must be exotic—that's what the word means. It is perhaps exotic to realize it.

Though it must be exotic, wonder is still a transformation, and all transformation is from one stage or way of being to another. The courageous are still afraid, the tourists still perceive the architecture, the extraordinary thinker still thinks. The origin is not dismissed entirely; that's why the term is "transformation" and not "transcendence" or "replacement" or "substitution." To think about the world and our own unique existence is not to leave the world, nor to separate ourselves from our concrete existence within it. We do not, when we wonder, or when we are transformed by art, leave our bodies and take up souls, nor do we put on magic cloaks that give us preternatural powers. Neither do we adopt a language of illusion, speaking mythically or superstiously in illegitimate ways, usurping the discourse of concrete testability to the unsanctioned uses of mysterious nonsense. Here is doubtlessly a challenge: in what way is the exotic achieved by legitimate transformation and not leaps into superstition? Even in this reflective question the twin but opposing dangers of anthropomorphism and reductionism threaten us; but the threat is not an ogre; we do know how to avoid it in both of its forms. Reason carries with it the critical defenses that allow us to see the dangers and, if not to overcome them entirely, at least to keep them at bay sufficiently so as not to surrender the exotic altogether, nor, by thinking of the exotic, to cut loose the origins of the common altogether. There is no guarantee in wonder, for we are, after all, wonderers precisely because we are finite, and so we can err in wonder as surely as we can err in common sense. What we are certain of is that, lacking wonder altogether, we are prone to deeper errors, errors that imprison us or reduce us or diminish us. To break out of a prison requires a violence, too. We are going to wonder whether or not we plan to; we are going to be transformed by fearing and by art, whether we want to be or not.

These preparatory reflections now allow us to make the suggestion that is the central insight or theme of this work, hinted in the fourth sketch. Philosophical wonder at its highest level has for centuries been denoted as metaphysics—a point that needs further analysis later—and metaphysics has usually been understood as the study of the real. The suggestion now is that metaphysics is a fundamental transition in our thinking; this transition is from ordinary thinking about ourselves and the world to extraordinary thinking, and only this latter enables us to confront directly our reality. An almost abandoned or overlooked problem, which now needs to be addressed, is the nature and meaning of this transition. We have seen glimpses: fear as a natural event is available to ordinary thinking; when confronted deeply, this fear is transformed to enable courage, and enablement can only be understood by extraordinary thinking, hence being courageous is metaphysically relevant. Fearing shows us how we react, possibly even why and how we react, but courage reveals our essence, our reality. The art of architecture transforms our contextual seeing into essentialist looking; the mere facts of a criminal case before a jury can be transformed by the suggestion of the word *loyalty* into a metaphysical understanding of the defendant's character, and thus possibly a different verdict.

This suggestion has one obvious consequence that seems to leap out at us as soon as it is made. If such transitions are understood metaphysically, then the range of that honorable discipline is hugely altered and grossly expanded. With regards to what constitutes the proper topics, Kant may seem the most parsimonious: he claims there can be only three: God, soul, and freedom. Contemporary analytic thinkers include a few more: the mind/body problem, freedom or determinism, the existence of an external world (!), the nature of truth, and once again, regressively, what is the ultimate stuff? This approach to metaphysics according to its topics serves the taxonomists extremely well, but disserves those who wonder critically. We cannot know in advance the whole list of what the topics are or what they should be; but we can realize that the profound transformation of our thinking must raise certain topics that do not seem to belong to the traditional list; and that even those topics on the traditional list must be reexamined on the basis of the fundamental transition in our thinking.

Whatever the topics are, even if they are prolix and elusive or traditional and fettered with bad analysis, an inquiry into philosophical transformation cannot proceed entirely without them; we realize only that topics cannot preexist and hence determine the inquiry; it is the other way around. With the suggestion that the very inquiry itself is transformational, one topic seems to emerge as deserving a preliminary reflection.

THREE

Being Real

Strictly speaking, the topic of metaphysical wonder is being real. The diction here must be stressed: the term "reality" is either an abstraction as "equality" is an abstraction from what is equal, or a collective, as "citizenry" is of citizens; and though it can be used legitimately, the dangers of its illegitimate use (especially that of reifying an abstraction) are considerable. To identify being real rather than reality as the single metaphysical topic is both safer and more truth revealing, though smoothness of syntax allows us to use the latter term, being forewarned. Further, the ineluctably real—though this is by no means obvious and certainly not self-evident—is our own *being* real, and not the "existence of external objects"—itself a dangerous locution. The ranking status of our own being real does not suggest solipsism or egocentric isolation, for being real includes being in the world. Indeed, the danger is entirely opposite. So easily available are the resources for learning about things in our environment, and so powerful is the uncritical persuasion that "reality" is to be found in, and even limited to, entities that are the object of our empirical knowledge, that the realization of our own being real becomes a rarified and possibly even wondrous achievement. To ask about the real is so privileged and profound that it is entirely unakin to any other species of inquiry. It is thus a wonder.

This may seem counterintuitive or even outrageous. What is so rare, so special, so wondrous about inquiry into our own reality—that is, our own being real? Surely it is simply an undeniable given: of course I exist! Who would deny it? Or if we prefer to reach into philosophical history, does not every student know of Descartes' *cogito ergo sum*? To inquire into our own being real is not at all the same as Descartes' consideration of the certainty of whether I exist. The present inquiry asks about our being real, not whether we exist, and certainly not the certainty *that* we exist. We are uncritically aware of our existence every day and in various ways, but rarely of our reality. Indeed, to be aware of anything as metaphysically real requires a special focus that requires transformation. As an example, we might reflect on suffering in many rich ways: how to endure it, avoid it, recognize its types, sympathize with those afflicted by it, trouble our minds about its justification, curse it, and realize the role it plays in the reflective adventures of the arts. Yet none of these worthy considerations confronts the reality of suffering—its metaphysical significance and the illusions inherent in denying it. To speak of suffering as real is to probe into the phenomenon as an irresistible part of our essence, an existential necessity that denudes our vulnerability as finite even as it transforms that vulnerability into a species of wonder that enables fundamental learning, and hence, truth. But if the reality of so common a condition as suffering is rarified, even more is the reality of our own being. To inquire into our own being real requires a special effort precisely because we are constantly faced not with our being *as* real, but our actual existence; not with our being *real* but with our being fragmented into our various functions: we label ourselves as subjects, agents, as bodies, as souls, as bundles of interests or egos seeking satisfaction or consumers needing the unnecessary, or as roles played in a hundred different games. If we are to transform our thinking from such labels to our own being real we must also realize that our being real seems perversely designed not to reveal itself, almost as if an essential part of being real is to hide or dissemble the very reality we seek to grasp. If our being real is itself a species of shyness or elusiveness, we must also ask why this is so.

What does it mean to be real? Our first instinct is to say that being real means not being a mere illusion or a mere appearance. I look at myself in the mirror and say: the image, though it exists, is not real; I am. Closely following this we say that being real entails a certain species of independence: I am not merely someone else's fantasy, nor am I a mere characteristic of a larger entity: I am not a predicate of something else. This is the Aristotlean inspiration that only being (*ousia*) can have predicates and never be a predicate of something else—an argument that gave rise to the unfortunate Latin translation from the Greek, *ousia*, into *substantia*. These preliminary steps are insightful but dangerous, for with the term 'substance' already the tendency is to look at something other than ourselves, such as a ball of wax, learn from it what independent substantiality means, and then reapply these discoveries to ourselves—which is exactly the procedure that is disallowed by the earlier realization I am directly conscious and not indirectly or inferentially conscious of being real. If I am not a characteristic or predicate of a larger, encompassing entity then neither can I be the mere product of smaller entities that in assemblage make up a construct—me—out of more fundamentally real, non-me building blocks. Thus my own reality as real cannot be the result of construction. That my reality might be a construct is entertained solely on the invalid technique of using nonpersonal, external entities as the basis for reality conceived as the fictive "external world." But I do not say the externals are real, *hence* I am, too—rather I say I am real *as* I am. I need not doubt the reality of other things, I merely disregard them. Indeed, to say *I* am real is to say I am nonreducible; this is why we conceive of the physical elements that make up my corpse as continuing to *exist*, but I, as real, am not present in my existing, future corpse. This reflection cannot be used, of course, to prove or disprove the existence of an incorporeal entity or soul.

To say I am real, in addition to being independent in some sense—at least sufficiently so as to realize I am not others—also must mean that as real I am the basis of what is true about me. The real is the ground of the true, but in reflective wonder that enables fundamental transformation, truth is the availability of the real, so that whatever is true must be true of the real. As a consequence of this realization, if profound learning about who and what I am provides *truth*—and all genuine learning is true—then what makes it true is my reality. Hence if it is true I can wonder, especially if I wonder about being true, it is true because my being real somehow enables it.

We now can see the importance of transformation. To inquire into our being real is not merely one among many possible inquiries; it requires not only a profound change in the manner or way in which we think, it also relies on a similarly profound change in our own being real. We are transformed from the decently clad to the shamefully denuded, not just from thinking about but being thought about—and this being thought about by our own thinking changes *what* is thought—we are transformed in our reality—that is, we become metaphysically different. Just as the brief but terrible realization of confronting our fear as courageous radically changes what fear means, so confronting our being real radically changes what *we* mean. Unlike the specific transformations such as courage and art, however, in the context of profound asking about our being real, no simple phenomenon will suffice. We ask: if to confront our reality is a transformation, from what and to what are we transformed? The formal answer is fairly easy to suggest: we are transformed from being unaware to being aware of our reality, and as a consequence, being real now matters and is thinkable in a way unavailable to the pretransformed modes of being; and more wondrously, the very reality of our being is itself transformed, somewhat akin to a secret being transformed into a nonsecret by being discovered, or an image in a mirror being transformed from an apparent second person until it is then recognized as a mere reflector. Yet the transformation of our own being to our being real is not merely perspectival as secrets and mirrors. We know of people who speak of personal epiphanies, as when a convert to a new religion changes his behavior and outlook to such an extent he speaks of himself as a new man; or when a believer experiences such huge and mindless evil that he rejects his faith in God altogether. In such cases it seems churlish not to accept the claims that such people have in some sense been transformed. Yet, in personal epiphanies of this sort one might protest that they have experienced profound *psychological*, and not *metaphysical*, changes. Perhaps; but mention of such epiphanies is not intended to see them as paradigms, but merely to show that profound alterations in our self-understanding have analogues. A more accurate comparison may be the transformation that occurs from being a child to being an adult—but that transformation is so fecund with metaphysical richness it needs a separate chapter. Before such analyses, however, the confusion about the metaphysical ultimate needs to be considered. Why do we ask about our reality, rather than our existence or our status as an entity?

When philosophers seek even to ask about what is fundamental, unfortunately they are met with a rather bewildering list of possibles; and what is worse, they find that most thinkers simply assume theirs is the only and obvious way to begin the inquiry. What term locates fundamental asking? Kant, for examples, argues that to say something exists is to say it is merely the object of possible experience; hence he denies pure reason can prove the existence of anything whatsoever; so it is not a surprise that reason cannot prove the existence of the soul or freedom or God. However, he does not deny that soul, freedom, or God may be thought as real. This ranks reality above existence. Heidegger argues that both existence and reality are subsumed under the more fundamental term, 'being'; furthermore, for Heidegger, existence means something entirely different from what it does for Kant or Descartes. In other traditions, especially the analytic epistemologists, the fundamental term seems to be the world, or possibly entities that either make up the world, or if the world is an entity too, are *in* the world.

It may seem that with this proliferation of possible ultimates or fundamental ways of asking, the thinker must simply rely on his own instincts or inheritance, and trust that his inquiry may discover whether how he asks is correct. Perhaps; but we need not be so impoverished. It is possible not merely to list the candidates that purport to be the way of setting the metaphysical problematic, but to do so in a taxonomic way, thereby providing a critical method for understanding what is entailed in each problematic—that is, how we raise the question—and with such understanding to evaluate them. The list need not be complete, but the dominating historical uses should be included. It must be stressed that what we are listing taxonomically are not metaphysical theories, as we might distinguish materialists from idealists or process metaphysics from entity-based accounts—for as important as such theories are, they are the answering products of thought, whereas the present list concerns the pretheoretic asking that determines how we set the problem up—the problematic—and hence how to answer it. There seem to be three major candidates; faced with the need to label them, the choice seems to be either to invent neologisms or to rely on traditional labels. Both have their drawbacks; but neologisms usually cause more confusion than enlightenment, and as long as the traditional terms are girded with predictable caveats, they seem more helpful. Accordingly I suggest dividing the fundamental problematics—that is, the pretheoretic, almost instinctive ways to ask—into three groups: (1) cosmological, (2) speculative, and (3) metaphysical.

1. The central and guiding terms for the cosmological problematic are the words *world* and *thing*. Variants of the first include: *universe, cosmos, creation*, and even such imprecise locutions as *everything*. The second cosmological term, "thing," also has variants: including *entity, substance, beings*, and on a more abstract level, *actuality*. The term "world" is the most dangerous of all philosophical usages, in part because it is so seductive and vague. It is seductive because it seems to function as an anchor or even ground: surely whatever exists belongs to, or even constitutes, the world. It is vague because it suggests too many different readings, especially the phrase 'external world,' as if the 'internal world' is to be dismissed entirely, or worse, to require an unbridgeable dualism between the two. Leibniz introduces the greatest proliferation of all time, assuring us of an infinity of possible worlds, which messes everything up terribly because the whole point in using the term "world" as the ultimate problematic is to include everything—even possibilities. Nevertheless, for Leibniz to suggest an infinity of possible worlds reveals how great the seduction is to use the word as the ultimate metaphysical anchor. Outside the world is nothing. Surely this is why Thales began the theoretical history of the cosmologists by assuring us the world was made of water. Even contemporary thinkers do not hesitate to invoke the world as the ultimate metaphysical problematic, asking: how are we to understand the world? They ask this question as if Kant had never existed.

It is the second of the cosmological problematics that seems to dominate what we quaintly call the "modern" period, with Descartes asking about things or substances. To suggest the world is simply the sum of all things is a profound inversion: which is more basic, thing or world? Which explains which? Is it simply a matter of the whole explaining the parts or the parts explaining the whole? Or does the immediacy of our consciousness support the Cartesian view that our own existence is inescapable, so this one thing, my own mind, must set the very vocabulary of all speculation? The Greeks begin with world, and from that beginning arrive at mind; Descartes and his followers begin with mind as an entity, and arrive at the world made up of three kinds: material, mental, and divine. It may seem that substantive metaphysical theories should not be equated with world-centered cosmologies, but Descartes' analysis of what a thing is relies on the external world, a ball of wax as an item in that world. Whether we begin with world and describe things in terms of it, or begin with things and deem the world to be merely the totality of such things, the fundamental problematic is still cosmological. Spinoza, after all, saw the point quite clearly: if you define thing as a substance, and insist substance is independent, there is little to stop you from realizing there can be only one substance, so the world is the thing and the thing is the world.

To initiate the metaphysical problem by asking either about the world or things externalizes the inquiry, often with disastrous results. We do want to know about the world and about things, and most of our daily concerns quite properly are directed by this problematic. Since metaphysics transcends the daily concerns for such matters, to initiate the inquiry by asking about them distracts from the unique role of fundamental inquiry. Perhaps the two greatest problems inherent in the cosmological problematic are the dread tendency to think of the ultimate as the *external*, that is, natural, world; and then, realizing the danger, to set up as a false problem the need somehow to relate the external to the internal, creating the most bogus of all issues, the mind/body problem.

2. The speculative problematic begins where the cosmological ends, shifting the mind/body problem to the mind/body beginning. Thus the key words are not *world* and *thing*, but *principle* and *system*. (By system I mean what enables coherence.) The thing becomes object, the world becomes the absolute, or the system that makes entities thinkable (in the sense of all that exists). If the danger of the cosmological problematic is to isolate us from or reduce us to the external world, the counterdanger of the speculative problematic is to equate what exists to how it is thought. There is decisive shift in this problematic to the epistemic as anchor. Rather than beginning with thing as a brute given, we define thing as the object of empirical consciousness: to be a thing is to be what is thought in terms of space, time, and causality. Yet, in spite of the seeming hegemony of the epistemic—what *is*, is determined by how I *think* it—the instinct to raise the ultimate question in terms of consciousness remains a metaphysical act. Although extreme or radical subjective idealists are rare, most thinkers whose original asking stems from our thinking do not deny the autonomous existence of entities outside us. It is more subtle than that. Ordinary dictionaries for example often define *metaphysics* as the study of the principles of ultimate reality, expecting the reader to focus on the last two words. It is somehow difficult for these lexicographers to suggest metaphysics studies reality itself. So why do they insert the term "principle," as if only principles can be studied? Even the term "study" shows a bias: metaphysics is a recognized, identifiable discipline within the academy. There is nothing wrong with this—there are metaphysicians in the academy—and since most studies require principles it seems innocent enough to identify peculiar principles that apply to reality. But arsonists and firefighters are not used to explain fire; it is the other way around.

Curiously, in spite of the epistemic bias of these thinkers, a central term almost equal to principle is "existence"—conceived as the abstraction of existences (or even: things that exist). They recognize to their credit that principles are never free-floating; they are always principles about something; and the emerging presupposition is they are about things that exist. But such existences are never to be thought independently of the principles that make them cohere. Do atoms exist? Does God? Do free wills exist? Do people exist? Whether something exists, or may exist, or cannot exist, or must exist, requires a system of coherence, including modal logic that inevitably requires principles, and these principles are more fundamental than the things they explain. The unity of principle with what exists gives the speculative problematic considerable prestige in recent centuries in part because of the analogue with mathematics (as principle) and science (as actual events;) though this prestige may be waning. What, though, is the difference between asking what exists and asking what are things, or even asking what is in (or constitutes) the world? Many thinkers quite happily intermix these terms, saying that whatever exists is thought as a thing and any thing is a thing because it exists in the world. The difference is elusive, perhaps, but nonetheless critical. If the world is the ultimate basis for questioning, entities or things exist because they are in the world; but if existence and principle are ultimate, the world is derived from such notions: it becomes a system of existing things. The cosmological problematic is externalist first and internalist second; the speculative problematic places how we think about things (through principles or systems) above what or whether the thing or world exists. That many great thinkers use both sets of terms does not undermine the primacy of the problematic; *how* they intermix them is determined by which way they use first. This does not mean a thinker cannot change his problematic; when he does, however, he usually recognizes it as a transformation. Further, as in the five sketches in Chapter One, it is a transformation occasioned by a simple word or words.

3. The metaphysical problematic, which alone of the three possibilities demands transformation, asks in one of two ways: the real or being. Since it is possible to suggest, as Kant does, that to say something exists is to say it is the object of possible experience, it is clear we need to entertain the possibility of another term that has greater extension. Kant's own suggestion is *reality*, which he distinguishes from appearance. More recently, however, Heidegger, adumbrated sketchily by Nietzsche, has shown that being—in the infinitival sense of asking what it means to be—is the fundamental problematic, and his reasoning and analysis are powerful. It is possible to conjoin them—what does it mean to be real?—and such conjunction may be the most fruitful way of asking. Both being and reality are here deemed as metaphysical problematics because asking about them places us in a curious position that straddles the inquiry and the inquirer. To ask about being or being real transforms the asker into the asking being asked. Among the ancients there are hints of this as early as Parmenides, Heraclitus, and Anaxagoras, but it is Plato who embraces the realization of it most fully; Kant and his nineteenth-century followers also sensed the importance of bringing the questioner himself directly into the problematic of metaphysical wonder; but it is Heidegger

who achieves the deepest significance of this inclusion by freeing the infinitival meaning of the term 'being' from the prison of its instantiation in the participle or gerund. We learn to think about what it means to be without first establishing the kind of entity we are or the entities that make up the world.

Heidegger's reflections show that even to express either cosmological or speculative problematics assumes the primacy of the various forms of the verb, *to be*. 'Whatever is, is a thing,' in order to be meaningful, must presuppose we have at least a vague understanding of the term *is*; further, since it is genuinely possible to ask what it means to be a father, a citizen, a dogcatcher or a thinker, it seems we can ask what it means simply to be at all. In this way all the traditional terms are brought under the same form of asking: what does it mean to be in the world? What does it mean to be a thinker (or what does it mean to think?) What does it mean to be a thing and for there to be things? The inclusion of traditional terms concerning the problematic is not in itself remarkable, for all three ways of asking can include the entire vocabulary of the others: rather it is the manner in which such asking provides a concrete but universal inquiry into the modalities of existence. I can ask directly what it means to take up space or to experience sensations without first instantiating a corporal entity, body; I can ask what it means to think, to reason, and to wonder, without first instantiating a mind. It may well be that having or even being a body is what is meant by sensing or feeling, but this merely shows such instantiation follows rather than precedes such reflection.

If Heidegger's success with these existential-ontological accounts places being as the fundamental problematic, why then persist with the term "real"? To ask what it means to be is not the same as to ask what it means to be real; the latter focuses our attention on three important addenda: the significance of being real as opposed to being appearance; the significance of reality as the basis of the true, the irrepracibility of the real. These three points must be examined further if we are to appreciate why only this conjoined problematic requires transformation; and since it does require transformation it reveals itself as the only fundamental way to ask what is ultimate.

To focus on being real rather than appearance may seem rooted in Kant's antimonic discoveries, and his distinction between phenomena and noumena that seems to follow from it. Kant, however, can be seen as briefly falling back to a discredited vocabulary, for faced with the need to account for the two, he uses the term "worlds." This is unfortunate, since reflection quickly shows us that by "world" Kant means "realm," or "way of thinking about," thereby cheating slightly on the expectation of the reader. It is more helpful, I think, to suggest that what drives us to consider distinguishing ourselves from mere appearance is the reductionism inherent in the latter designation, hence adding irreplacibility to nonappearance and truth-grounding. What is suggested in the term "real" as opposed to appearance is precisely the notion of nonreduction: I simply cannot be explained by, nor can I think about myself solely with regard to, whatever explains anything other than myself. If by 'appearance' we substitute the notion of being explained by whatever explains external entities, then to explain myself as appearance is to explain everything about me *except* myself.

If to be real means not to be fully explained in terms of other kinds of entities, then are we not marooned on an island of solipsism? Is it not precisely to avoid such isolation that we rely on nonprivate anchors such as the world, principles of coherence, God, external entities, or even things? For this surely becomes the crux: if I am real, and by being real I mean in part not being explained by terms that refer to some external anchor beyond me, then am I not truly a monad, an alien, an irrational and unsharable thwarter to all coherence? The agony of this realization offers only a painful disjunction: either I am entirely accountable by nonprivate factors, in which case I lose my uniqueness as fundamentally real, or I am uniquely real, in which case I am sundered from the world and others by an unbridgeable gap. Neither suggestion appeals; both offer their own legitimate demands. If I am real, I am radically alone; if I am not alone, I belong to and am ultimately reduced to, something other than myself. This is a cruel disjunction.

It may be cruel, but it is truth, not disjunction, that is its essence. It is precisely because of this realization that to be real is to be able to be transformed. There is something precious in what might be called the existential solipsism: my life, my existence, is beyond copy. Never before, in all history prior to my birth, was there this being I call myself; never again, after my death, will there be me. No one, now or ever, is me except myself; my brief, unique, finite, frightened, and bewildered life begins and ends. Unbidden torments seep like the stench of sepulchers into my weary brain; utterly precious heaves of private joys, knowable only to me are mine alone. Because of this uniqueness, I matter—indeed I matter absolutely. Who would deprive us of these our secret private cores that sustain us like fundamental food? Or perhaps these private, unsharable centers do not sustain but abandon, they are not existential nutrients like food but nihilistic poisons that offer death by cutting off the oxygen of communal life. Perhaps they are both; they poison and sustain. But whatever they are, they cannot be denied, not if truth matters.

Yet this isolation is curiously necessary for dwelling in the world. These inward secrets are entirely mine; yet they echo in the arts, surprise us in their revelations of genius, shadow us in the shared lives of others: we share only because we are unsharable—this is not a contradiction but an enlightening paradox: only as lonely can I reach to succor and suck another's abandonment into my own. To be dreadfully alone—and to be forced to the realization of it—is what enables sharing. This realization is a transformation. The feared is an external threat; but to face it is the loneliest, most intimate confrontation, for no one but us can do it—only we can originate our courage; no one else can be courageous for us. Yet when fundamental thinking enables truth, our own private being is transformed into a sharing that is dearer just because it is true. The real is the ground or origin of the true; our reality cannot be shared but the truth of our reality can be. Our nonsharable reality (being real as unsharable) is transformed into sharable, i.e., learnable, truth.

If this suggestion is even partly right, the nature and meaning of such transformation becomes the supreme metaphysical issue. Transformation in this existential, metaphysical sense is not explained in terms of certain psychological feelings—though wonder, as is noted in the prior chapter, seems to qualify in a way—rather, to transform is to confront the confronted or think the thinker is such a way as to render the reality of the confronted so as to be enabled to confront as it is confronted. In short, we transform reality into truth. A special caveat must here be noted: this is neither the problem of "other minds" nor bridging the gap from an isolated mind to the external world. Nor is it a one-time event that forever alters the outlook of the thinker, as a religious conversion might do. Transformation is entirely unlike the pseudoproblems of speculative theories because there is no original postulation of one kind of entity, mind, over and against another entity, the world. It may be better to think of transformation verbally, as transforming or to transform. If to transform is to render our being real as truth, and not merely the *result* of such rendering as a species of knowledge, or even a completed act, then wonder is of its essence. Not only is wonder the essence of such rendering or of such an act, we must now realize that the epistemological concerns shift as well. In a move that must surely irritate if not outrage traditional epistemologists, the definition, criteria, and processes of knowledge must be replaced by what is more original: not knowing but learning. This suggests learning is not achieving knowledge, but quite the contrary; knowledge is understood in terms of learning. I know only because I have learned. Knowledge is the finished product: it is the footprint in the sand, occasioned by, and hence derived from, the more original act of walking on the beach. When this learning transforms our own unshared reality into the sharable, though not reducible, manifestation in truth, we achieve metaphysical wonder, but this wonder now takes on the character of a learning that transforms. We learn truth. Whatever is known is, of course, true; but this realization is about a finished product, a proposition that somehow refers or tells us about what is already learned. Learning is not of true propositions, for such propositions can be called true only after they are learned *as* true. Knowledge, if conceived apart from learning, is akin to being told the final score of the championship game, without watching or thrilling to the actual game itself. But he who knows only the final score cannot be said to realize the truth of the game as played. We learn philosophical or existential truth only when we realize truth is reality violently transformed, as courage and art can be seen as our own being real transformed into truth by a self-confronting violence.

To suggest philosophical truth is violently transformed reality may seem an indulgence. Yet, the problem is ancient and persistent. What is the relation between truth and reality, especially if we ourselves are real? How can I share my own reality if I am nonreducible? How can I be of worth if I am reducible? If these are indeed ancient questions, as they surely are, they suggest that the elusive relation between truth and reality itself must be thinkable in a manner somewhat akin to what is here designated as transformational violence.

FOUR

Violence

It is always dangerous to cheapen terms by ubiquitous expansion, especially those that denote violence. To describe a brief fracass between children on the playground as warfare demotes the impact of genuine international carnage; an unwelcome pat on the back censured as rape trivializes the horror of true sexual felony; to devote as tragic the loss of a replaceable bauble emasculates the term applied to *King Lear.* What could be less violent than a civil discussion of professors in a seminar room, with wine and cheese, belaboring an obscure point about Anaximander? The discussion may be defended as a contribution to academic research, but to suggest there might be violence in such respectful disputation may seem to devalue the term. The noun is rooted in the verb, so what is violated? Not all academic discussions about philosophical theories or issues are violent; perhaps most are not. There may yet be, though, genuine violence in certain philosophical acts, but the burden is on the affirmation, and the distinctions are important. If every remark, critique, or analysis by all writers in any form that touches on the subject of reality are deemed violent, then trivialization demeans the claim. The suggestion being considered in this chapter is not that a few wild theories can be found in the works of original thinkers, but only that profound reflection on what it means to be real is violent thinking, that violence lies in the very nature of such thinking, and that this violence transforms who we are.

If violence violates, what, in thinking on being real, is violated? It would be glib and disingenuous to offer as a response that the violated are the prior metaphysical reflections of unenlightened thinkers, as if an analogy were made to revolutions overthrowing the *ancien régimes.* Nor would it mean very much to suggest that what is violated is ignorance, or even the banality of the everyday tedium of the thoughtless. We might come closer to what is meant if we suggest that we ourselves are the violated, just as we are the violators;

but even if this suggestion contains a worthy insight the offering is so raw, in the sense of uncultivated, it means little without refinement. It is neither arbitrary nor glib to suggest thinking about our own being real—the seminal origin of all metaphysics—is violent; and this requires that the nature of violence itself must be raised.

The broken dam releases the huge energy of a town-destroying cascade, so sudden and immense that the citizens can do nothing about it: seeing it crash down on them, they know they are going to die. The invasion of a vast enemy host upon the unprepared is unstoppable; the huge phalanx of tanks overweens our small army of trucks and rifles; there is nothing the people can do to halt the irresistible onslaught; we are defeated. The eruption of the volcano, even if no one is imperiled, fills the safely distant observer with an awesome sense of impotence: here is so much power, so much ungoverned energy, one can only submit to its undeniability. In such cases, violence seems to suggest an indifference to our will and control; it is destructive of all that is planned, arranged, and designed; its force is irresistible, and the experience of it starkly denudes our vulnerability and impotence. Yet . . .

We watch and hear the enormous thrust as the rocket spears its way toward a seeming vulnerable sky, forcing itself beyond the puny restraints of planetary gravity and even local space itself. Yet it is our design; we built it and want the launch to happen and seem to thrill to the conquest over mere nature inherent in our engineering. That the rocket is using natural energy and is made of natural elements in no way distracts us from this sense of dominion over the natural, over the earth, over the world, even. The enormity of its power may entitle the event as violent; yet it is controlled and guided, making it seem, in some sense, not truly violent; for what, in the flight of a modern rocket, is violated? Perhaps the violated is nature in the sense of what is undisturbed by human influence. We noted the invading army as seeming violent; but to the enemy commanders the power is all the more important for its being controlled, willed, planned, and successful. Is the invasion violent only to the conquered, and merely controlled power to the conquerer?

When we speak of a violent man we seem to be saying that he is strong-willed, perhaps unstable, ready to use brute and physical strength to achieve his ends. We may also be suggesting a lack of self-control, as in one quick to anger, often characterized with the finely crafted phrase: short-tempered. What we do not mean, however, is simply that the man has extraordinary physical strength, for we do not label a gentle giant as violent; indeed occasionally the violent are themselves relatively puny, even physically weak, but overcompensating for these shortcomings by intense rage or callous indifference to others. If the gentle giant has power or energy but is not violent we cannot equate the adjectives. The key seems to be either the intensity of will to the exclusion of others, or the lack of control over one's own passions.

There seems, however, to be a less frequent but still positive sense to violence, above all in the creative act within the arts, especially when we speak of originality. Thus musical genius such as found in Bach, Mozart, and Wagner is often credited with altering forever the history of its art, and thus is violent both in the sense of creating something new and lasting, and in the sense of conquering the hegemony of the older forms. There is a biblical injunction that the kingdom of heaven suffereth violence and only the violent shall bear it away, suggesting at the very least that goodness is not merely passive, that acts such as sacrifice and martyrdom involve an inner power that dominates rather than yields. Even in these rarified cases however, violence does not mean possessing mere strength or energy, but requiring a fierce will to active dominance over the normal and the ordinary. In literature, especially poetry, love is often depicted as violent, not in the sense of simply succumbing to lust, but in the wrenching torment and ecstatic joy that seem to recast the entire universe. These positive senses of violence, however, may seem at first merely metaphoric or analogic, for if violence violates it is difficult to see it as favorable, since the violated must be deemed as dear or precious in order for its being overcome or conquered to matter.

Positive—that is, worthwhile—violence need not be so blithely dismissed. The violated must be dear or even precious, so there is a sense of loss in all violence, but it does not follow that nothing can outrank the worth of the violated: life itself may be both dear and precious, but the violence of sacrificial martyrdom can still be endorsed as positive, not only because of the esteem given to that for which or for whom the sacrifice is made, but also because of the qualities necessary to bring it about, such as courage and loyalty. Courage can often be seen as violent, as when huge spiritual energy violates something precious and dear, such as security or even life itself, for the sake of something greater. Worthwhile or positive violence is therefore possible, but always at a price. Something dear must be violated, for without the violated there is no violence. Even in the cases of positive violence, however, there is suggested the sense of irresistability and conquest, and to a lesser extent, the loss of control and order.

Perhaps the term "violence" should be used to describe natural events, however devastating, only as a metaphor, restricting literal violence to willful acts. This would emphasize the notion that to violate is willfully to damage, harm, or destroy another person through the use of force. Rape, war, beating someone senseless, bombing buildings in terrorist attacks, and child abuse, rather than exploding volcanoes, would then seem to be paradigms of violence. A powerful weightlifter would thus be strong but not violent, whereas a penalty-prone linebacker or punitive hockey player would be violent because each seeks to damage and harm the opposing player, considering it praiseworthy to watch the fallen stretchered off the field. Though one cannot prescribe usage, the stricture is in fact reinforced by the etymology and classical usage of the term.

After all, among the first original entries in the Oxford English Dictionary are those that refer to violations inherent in breaking an oath or a law, so that to violate a promise is more fundamental than for a river to "violate" its banks in a flood. Rape seems the paradigm of violence, not only because it violates the law, but because the brutal will of the rapist violates the victim of what is intimate and precious, thereby degrading and not merely injuring the raped. The enormity of the outrage also terrorizes, so that the victim is not only abused but so shamed by the intrusion as to reluct taking legal action, for the publication of the crime demeans both perpetrator and victim. The usurpation short of war of one country by another's troops is often metaphorically described as rape, as when we speak of Hitler's rape of Austria or Russia's rape of the Baltic republics: they were not only conquered, but shamed, in part because it was terror rather than actual war that usurped their sovereignty.

With these brief reflections, we must now ask in what sense is metaphysical reflection on being real violent? The four elements that seem necessary for violence are the sense of apparent irresistibility coupled to our impotence, the lack of governance or control, the vastness of the power involved, and the sense of the dear or precious being usurped. There may be a fifth: that violence is perspectival of the violated, not the violator. Unless the first four elements are present in some way, the caveat at the opening of this chapter must be enforced: it would be an emasculation to designate the transformation inherent in thinking on our own being real as violent. Indeed, if the caveat holds, only violence can transform being real to the truth of being real.

Reflections on certain qualities in truth itself may offer a few preliminary implements that, like pitons, are driven into the cliff by the climber prior to scaling it. Those who seek the truth even in ordinary matters realize that it is sometimes brutal to suspend our preferences and prejudices in order to allow truth to outrank belief and opinion. It may not yet be violent, but surely one meaning to truth in ordinary inquiries is its irresistability. The investigator who strongly believes a certain miscreant to be guilty, reluctantly finds the gathering evidence points to another who may be a friend. The scientist may set up an experiment to show his hypothesis is correct finds rather a new, perhaps unwelcome, hypothesis must be entertained. This is partly what is meant by the word *truth*: it is independent of our preference, and the methods of uncovering it seem to possess a relentless inevitability about its disclosure. This independence of our preference or even planning need not yet suffice to qualify as violent, but, like the piton in the rock, it offers a handhold. However, ordinary inquiry, though it seeks topical truth, is not violent per se; it takes on pseudoviolent characteristics only if the discovery is unexpected or undesired reactions that are mere psychological feelings rather than metaphysical transformations. The independence of truth from such feelings, sometimes dangerously noted as "objectivity," does, however, provide an analogical sense of irresistibility, and hence may be heuristically helpful.

If there is violence in the transformation from reality to truth, and reality here is seen as our own being real, both the violence itself and the violated must be understood in terms of inner turmoil. It does not seem far-reaching to suggest that most if not all species of inner turmoil are violent. Analogies within the broader classification may then be suggested. We speak, for example, of the (violent) inner turmoil inherent in the conflict between loyalty to a friend and our duty as a citizen, or between our oath to enforce the law and our broader sense of justice, as Captain Vere endures the torment of judging the sweet innocent, Billy Budd. These are not merely psychological feelings; there is a real conflict that burdens us as thinkers. Inherent in such cases is the agonizing realization that we cannot escape the burden: not to act is itself an action with consequences. The problem is exacerbated by the realization of its universality: Vere must confront his own demons in terms of the transcendent conflict between the need for law and the need for justice. It is precisely because both have legitimate claims upon us that renders the torment so unendurable. In such cases of moral, inner torment we note the four elements of violence: Vere cannot escape the burden, it is irresistible; nor is he entirely in control, though he is still responsible; the power of his command as well as the power of fate that fetters him to his dire predicament are both vast—they eclipse all possibility of small or clever maneuvers; and either way he judges, something very precious is violated, either Billy's life or the sacredness of his martial oath. We seem on firm ground then to suggest that inner turmoils not only can and do happen, they can also be violent. The question, then, may now be helpfully reformulated: is the search for truth about our own being real itself an inner turmoil? At first glance it seems that such searching cannot be an inner turmoil, for it is difficult to see what is violated. In the previous chapter, however, a cruel dilemma was revealed: to explain myself in terms other than myself removes me from the equation; to explain myself uniquely isolates me radically from the rest of the world. This dilemma reveals itself as violent when we recognize that belonging in the world is dear, but being unique is precious. I seem to want to explain myself in public terms, for what else is explanation except an appeal to what is publicly available? Yet I seem to realize that such public explanations by necessity must avoid precisely that which is unique to me. Further, there is a sense in which, even if the private were capable of being made publically available, to do so would be to denude me in a way that uncovers what is meaningful only as covered. Perhaps I am unique only until I reveal myself. Yet the inversion also fascinates: perhaps I am unique only when I am revealed.

In the first dialogic sketch of the opening chapter, the frightened youth endures not only the inner torment of two conflicting fears, but also his anguish is exacerbated by the presence of the other interlocutor: he feels not only the torment itself, but also the shame in the disclosure of the torment to another. Yet paradoxically the presence of the other may well enable his

courage. Without the other, the youth may not be able to discover the truth
of his being able to face himself; yet with the other he cannot avoid shrinking
from a disclosure, the manifestation of which is costly. There seems a paradox: sharing his torment verbally enables his courage, yet it is his courage that
maroons him from sharing it; to share it verbally shames him, but the shame
in a way extracts the courage like a tooth. It is possible, then, to suggest that
in some cases, courage is a species of self-realization in which the linguistic
articulation of the anguish inherent in it is not a mere addendum but a
necessary part of its essence. Language itself is part of the violence that
wreaks a self-realization that is essential for learning what it means to be real.
In this sense the dialogue is not merely *about* courage, it is a *part* of it—
namely, that part which, in rendering it open or available, also enables it. This
violent rendering it open as it enables it is truth.

    What must be deeply thought is the asking about the violated. Surely
something is violated as the youth agonizes over his courage, else there would
be no torment, and hence no inner violence. If the prior paragraph is even
close to the matter, it seems that truth itself is violent in that it rips open the
secret of our being real. This ripping open is not merely a revelation to those
other than ourselves, it reveals itself first and foremost to our own reluctant
probing. At the very least, then, what is violated is our reluctance; and this
reluctance is not based on some further consequence or subsequent loss, but
is built into our own being real. There must be a sense, then, in which being
real necessarily relucts to being revealed, so that the philosophical search for
truth is not a natural act, as curiosity might be. Perhaps the autonomy or
uniqueness of our own reality is precisely what resists being discovered, for
once it is brought out into the open, its power as secret and unique dissipates.
There is a suspicion, however, that this power inherent in secrecy is itself a
species of self-deceit or even self-eclipse: keeping it hidden keeps it feckless.
Whichever way we turn in this search for the violated, the paths before us
seem but traps.

    Is it possible, then, that the violence consists precisely in the inescapability
of this paradox? The violence is neither in our private being nor our public
disclosure but in being forced to wed them together. What is violated would
then be not the preciousness of the inner, nonshareable self, but that which
disjoins being real from being revealed; the wall, or perhaps better, the shield
that keeps truth apart from our reality is violated; without the shield we are
unprotected and denuded. With this diction the violence of being stripped
naked evokes the paradigm of the person-to-person violence of rape. Bringing together our own being real with its discovery would thus be akin to
bringing the rapist to his victim: it not only produces subsequent violence in
the actual raping itself but it violates both law and decency.

    Is this not too strong? The suggestion that metaphysical truth is violent
is meaningful only if it is positive or worthwhile, which felonious rape can

never be. Yet the metaphor of rape is too revealing to shun as a metaphor altogether; metaphysical thinking is violent in the sense of forceful intrusion into what is sacred in our privacy, even if it can, unlike rape, be thought of as positive or worthy. It may further seem counterintuitive to suggest that we are both the violated and the violator, but this, too, has its parallels, as when we read of medieval self-flagellants or those who torment themselves with oppressive guilt. To think about our own being real is to be violent to ourselves. It must be stressed that this violence is not caused by the discovery of a truth we did not want to learn, as a patriot may wince when discovering the cruelty in his country's history, but is owing to the very nature of the metaphysical act itself. To say we are violated is to say we suffer, but the suffering inherent in the act of thinking on our own being real is not because we learn something that counters what we previously believed or even what we prefer, but that the thinking itself is a species of suffering, just as one might say the heart aches (suffers) in the very act of loving, which is itself a joy.

To suggest a parallel between the ache of joyous loving to the phenomenon of metaphysical truth being violent is not without great precedent, especially that of Plato's depiction of the erotic Socrates. It may serve us well to reflect on this precedent, not in the sense of seeking support for the present analysis, but to learn from a greater mind. In addition, it may prove fruitful to extend the historical precedents briefly to include both Kant and Heidegger who also appeal to violence inherent in thinking; but for the moment, it is Plato's Socrates who seems to intrude himself into these reflections almost as a demand, for who else trumpets the anguish of erotic longing as an essential part of the philosophical act?

When one thinks of the role eros plays in the Socratic dialogues, the *Phaedrus* and the *Symposium* come readily to mind; and why not? These two dialogues have eros as their theme, and have so interwoven themselves into the literature of the Western canon that they rise up in the mind as masked children on Halloween, knocking on our doors, demanding they be seen and favored. It were folly to disregard them; but it may also be folly to approach them as the sole resources, especially if they are taken as providing mere theories about love. It may, then, be advantageous to reflect first on the more general role that eros seems to play even in dialogues whose themes are not specifically about the erotic. The issue is obviously a dicey one, for the subject matter is itself not without controversy. There are two dangers to avoid: the reader or scholar must not try to sanitize the dialogues to make them palatable to modern sensibilities; but neither should these works be seen as endorsing a vulgar praise of mere lust, hailing the contemporary endorsement of promiscuous indulgence. Eros is, was, and always shall be a deeply disturbing phenomenon, just because it is not the same as mere lust—or as the prevalent argot has it, "sex"—but neither is it the same as the loftier notions of marital security and devotion or Christian charity. Socrates himself should not be canonized in the sense that his character be seen as the paradigm of the virtues or even as a puritan's model of what a saint is supposed to be. That Socrates is a paradigm of one struggling not only with understanding the virtues but achieving them is obvious; that he represents a model of achieved virtue, including wisdom, is not. He is clearly attracted to young men and even boys; whether he is actively intimate with them is less clear, though some dialogues seem to suggest he is, other dialogues suggest he may not be. It is tempting to account for this merely in terms of historical anthropology, pointing out that the Athenian culture of that era was fairly liberal with regard to men having boys as lovers, and since no or little shame or guilt was attached to such relations, it is really a rather minor issue whether Socrates was sexually active with his male interlocuters or not. Athens was not as blatantly overt about this as the intensely conservative and militant Sparta, where very young boys were handed over to seasoned veterans, for the sake of producing an intimacy among the warriors that made then so effective as an army. These anthropological observations may help the reader but they may distract from the issue of Socratic eros. For the problem is not the mere acceptability, moral or social, of certain behavior; the question is how we are to understand the role of eros in Socratic philosophical thinking.

The dialogue *Charmides* concerns the virtue the Greeks called *sophrosone*: self-control, knowing one's place and one's role, and decorum. It is an irony that in a dialogue concerning self-control, Socrates enters a classical version of a gymnasium, asks about boys beautiful in body and soul, and then peeks into the briefly open garment of one, and is aroused by the boy's carnal beauty. Socrates manages to control himself so as to carry out the inquiry, but as the dialogue comes to an end, a highly ambiguous repartée ensues that suggests Socrates will no longer "resist" the beauty of the lad, Charmides. As a dramatic device it serves brilliantly to show what is at stake in the virtue of self-control and decorum: Socrates is indeed aroused, but his control of it provides a magnificent instantiation of the very virtue being considered. The possibility that the final exchange also shows that the control is not meant to be absolute; rather that there is a time and place fitting for certain things suggest that part of what *sophrosone* means is control, not denial, of passion. This adds a lively and vivid dramatic coda to the entire discussion, enabling us to appreciate how the content of the dialogues echoes its form. There is much to be said for such reading. However, the very fact that eros plays a role in philosophical discourse at all is of greater importance. Perhaps the very inquiry could not take place were Socratic invulnerable to the green, venereal beauty of the charming adolescent. Is it merely irony, or a more profound sense of beauty's violence that enables Socratic inquiry? These questions must be briefly shelved, lest they seem attached only to this one dialogue.

A far more serious matter is the dialogue *Lysis*, which is putatively concerned with friendship, not eros. Yet, the dialogic drama itself seems scandalous, if not shameful, for in it Socrates agrees to help the young man Hippothales seduce the tender boy Lysis, an agreement that in itself is bad enough, for Socrates actually abets the conquest of a boy so young that even the liberality of Athens might find it shameful. A thousand times worse, however, is Socrates' suggestion that the best way to seduce the boy is through philosophy, thereby transforming the love of truth into a pimp. This is not some fantastic, wild misreading of the text: Socrates clearly states that his intention is to show that Hippothales' present wooing of the boy with bad verses and songs is doomed to failure—that is, the boy will not be conquered by such tactics—but that Socrates' own gentle chiding of the boy's reasoning about friendship is meant as a technique to win the affection of the child: this is the way Hippothales should woo him. The outrage at this abuse both of child and philosophy immediately drives the scholars and critics to take refuge in disclaimers: all this prostitution of philosophy is an example of Socratic irony: Socrates only pretends to be helping Hippothales; actually he is helping Lysis resist the older youth by turning his attention away from eros and toward philos, away from seduction and toward dialectic. Irony, or rather putative irony, is the ultimate refuge for any reader made uncomfortable by what he reads. Furthermore, the natural and radiant friendship between the two boys, Lysis and Menexenus, first presented to us as one of those exquisite attachments of youth, is rendered as passing or shallow: Socrates intrudes himself between them, as the proverbial alienator of affection, replacing himself as Lysis' true friend, rather than Menexenus. In addition to prostituting philosophy as a whoremonger, he shatters a healthy, enviable friendship, transforming Lysis from a happy child into a doubt-ridden and insecure boy, led away by slaves. How can we make sense of such a seeming scandalous dialogue?

A certain toughness here redeems where appeals to irony merely emasculate. Truth matters; Socrates does care about Lysis, and deems it a greater friendship to offer shared dialectic as the union of true friendship with true inquiry. He also cares about Hippothales and even Menexenus; but for Socrates shared inquiry into truth is simply the greatest friendship possible, and it seems only Lysis grasps the point. But what about eros? Here the need for toughness as a resource for truth is even greater: Socrates does not condemn Hippothales' erotic longing, but merely his tactics to achieve it. The erotic is a necessary part of this curious and troubling dialogue, for it is the erotic that drives both Socrates and Hippothales into the conspiracy, and even as the dialogue ends with Socrates offering a more profound sense of friendship to the consternation of Menexenus, the erotic is still a palpable presence. The "end" of the dialogue, as aporetic, does not provide answers as closures, but what might be called provocative confusion on a deeper level; that is, we become more confused just because we are genuinely learning.

The presence of eros in the background can also be found in Book V of the *Republic*, in the *Ion*, and the *Euthydemus;* perhaps in other dialogues as well. Indeed, whenever the capital forms are mentioned, beauty is usually among them, and one's approach to beauty is almost always presented as erotic. This raises the question: is Socrates' approach to truth necessarily erotic? If beauty is the dominant form, perhaps the image suggests that philosophy is the erotic love of truth in the sense that we continually long and ache for that which we do not completely possess; indeed, given the choice perhaps the genuine lover of truth as beautiful would prefer a certain distance so as to intensify the longing, even as the longing itself is so great that conquering and possessing the beloved approaches a species of madness. Thus, erotic violence is inherent in the very nature of the inquiry. To see the justification for this, we need to turn to the two dialogues on love.

Central to the *Phaedrus* is the suggestion of the three-part soul revealed in the tripartite image of the chariot: the dark, lusty horse; the white, noble horse; and the struggling charioteer. Were the first horse entirely unharnessed, he would simply be raw desire, taking all that his strength would permit, satisfying his urges only long enough to reestablish ever new longings, a mere appetitive beast; but once yoked to the chariot, he becomes a necessary passion, for without his strength, and indeed vision—for it is only he who spots the beloved as beautiful—the chariot could not approach what it desires, neither the lovely youth nor, by metaphoric inference, truth itself. The present inquiry is spared the necessity of a precise analysis of each element; it is enough to recognize that the erotic love of the beautiful youth and the erotic longing for truth are both profoundly violent. It is not only the unruly horse, but indeed both the charioteer and the white horse who also must struggle with extreme energy and even desperate strength to keep the three forces unified. The violence is inherent in the entire metaphor; it is not the point to condemn the violence as a mere flaw inherent in our nature, but to praise it; for without it, both boys and truth would escape entirely.

This is reiterated in the *Symposium*. Agathon is asked by Socrates whether eros is the possession or the lack of that which is beautiful, and the young tragedian is daunted by the question, for he realize as soon as it is asked that either answer seems to excise the possibility of eros altogether. If I have the beloved, I no longer long; if I long for it, I cannot have it. This dilemma is then itself magnificently transformed from a seeming misological threat to a glorious realization of its essence. To love is to lack and possess at the same time. When Juliet confesses to Romeo at her balcony, she muses: "And yet, I wish but for the thing I have:/ my bounty is as boundless as the sea,/ My love as deep, the more I give to thee/ The more I have, for both are infinite." (act 2, scene 2) She lacks even as she possesses, and this inner turmoil is violent.

Few, it seems, would deny erotic violence; but what has this to do with metaphysical thought? For Socrates, everything. We neither have nor lack wisdom; we are always in between. What stuns us is the realization that Socrates embraces this paradox as the essence of thought itself: the unexamined life literally is not worth living; what gives life its meaning or worth is our examination of it. The aporia of the dialogues is essential: we do not even want to arrive at a propositional definition, for that would end the search. Yet few readers deny that they learn much about courage from reading the *Laches* and much about piety from reading the *Euthyphro*; so the search is not a static suspension, as if hanging exactly in the middle between two extremes is somehow wise. The longing is erotic, which means it is the unreachable but approachable beauty of truth, not the ultimate possession of it; and this endless longing must be assumed if the dialogic approach to inquiry is to avail our violent nearing of what is beloved in truth. To think, as a lover of truth, is thus violent.

Philosophical violence is not restricted to love-maddened Greeks with lax sexual mores; as rigorous and analytically profound a thinker as Kant places violence right in the center, as well as right at the beginning, of his entire critique. The very first sentence in the Preface of the first edition to *The Critique of Pure Reason*, translated by Norman Kemp Smith, assures us that human reason "has this peculiar fate" that it is forced, by dint of reasoning itself, to raise questions it cannot answer. This overture may seem a mere warning against speculative metaphysics until the reader arrives at the unexpected violence of the Antinomies. Reason's quest necessarily brings it to the speculative contradictions that must be affirmed in its thesis and antithesis. Not only are the antinomies themselves violent in the sense that, left unexamined, they must result in the misological defeat, but Kant assures us that this threat necessitates a further act of supreme, dialectical violence: rending our own reality in twain, forever disjoining ourselves as phenomena from ourselves as noumena in a manner that wrenches us cruelly apart. It is sheer violence on the part of reason itself that confronts the contradictions, embraces them as a purgative, and creates an entirely new way of thinking. It is the violence, and not the distinction itself, that is so remarkable. After all, in 1714, sixty-seven years before Kant published the *Critique*, Leibniz points out in §81 of the *Monadology* that bodies act according to efficient causes *as if there were no souls*, and souls act according to final causes *as if there were no bodies*. Here we have the original discovery: we think differently about different topics, thereby establishing two distinct realms that, internally at least, disregard the other. The Kantian realms of phenomena and noumena are adumbrated by Leibniz's distinction between two different causal explanations, efficient and final. For Leibniz, however, the difference is conjoined in an entirely peaceful, even gentle metaphor: harmony. For Kant, the difference is seen as warlike, violent, even romantically thrilling. His normal style, diction, and syntax, so well suited for the painstaking sloughing through the prodigious critique of human faculties, in the passages reflecting on the antinomies becomes positively eloquent, bold, and daring—it is an activist role, a leap into unchartered realms, a realization that reason *creates* a new role for itself: antinomic dialectic. One need only reflect briefly on the subsequent history to see how violent this dialectic truly is: Hegel, Fichte, Schopenhauer, even Nietzsche—and from Nietzsche to another thinker of violence, Heidegger. In the *Introduction to Metaphysics*, Heidegger seems almost to enshrine violence as a sacred precinct for philosophy. Early in that remarkably popular but deeply disturbing book, Heidegger transforms the traditionally irritating question asked by the parents of students: "What can you do with philosophy?" to the inverted and more probing form, "What can philosophy do to you?" This may seem a merely clever riposte; but we soon learn that Heidegger means to ask the question in terms of its awesome presupposition: philosophy, if done properly, violently transforms who we are. In his famous rendering of the speech by Chorus from *Antigone*, he points out that the opening lines are richly ambiguous. In Ralph Manheim's Translation (p. 147) they read: "There is much that is strange, but nothing that surpasses man in strangeness." The Greek word for "strangest," *deinotaton*, is also the word for the most violent or terrible. After this provocative opening, the speech lists many of the achievements of great men, from conquering the earth with the plow to building cities and armies, thereby conquering both nature and other men. The key to this violent strangeness seems to be language itself, which grounds wind-swift understanding and the establishment of authority. These violent upheavals are both good and bad, but in the end, man cannot conquer death. In the final lines of the piece, Chorus disassociates himself from such violence found in the heroic and the great, saying that such men are not welcome in his house. Even in the Sophoclean original, the speech is troubling and moving: we are strange even to ourselves, we have produced both great and terrible things, and we realize fate seems peculiarly pernicious to those who achieve grandeur, so that like Chorus, who is the paradigm of common thinking, we seek distance from them even as we admire them, although in our case this separation is provided by aesthetic removal. It is Heidegger's focus on power, however, that renders his reading so revealing. Is this the deepest way to understand ourselves, admitting our own strangeness and the violence inherent in being able to speak? Or has the voice of Chorus, in a remarkable irony, achieved a violent understanding that surpasses that of kings, namely the essence of man himself?

If it is man himself who is violent, however, what has this passage to do with the transformation inherent in philosophical thinking? Heidegger's analysis takes place in the section entitled "Thinking and Being" in which he examines what it means to be in terms of what it means to think and speak. Poetry and philosophical language are the supreme linguistic powers precisely because they reveal existential truth; only through language in its most violent forms, poetry and philosophy, can the truth of our own being be wrested from the choruslike tendency to keep our meaning hidden from ourselves.

The three figures, Plato, Kant, and Heidegger, thus provide precedents to the violent nature of philosophical inquiry, especially with regards to our own mystery. In their own ways, each also provides a sense of why violence is needed, and hence indirectly what is violated. For Plato, it is the erotic love of beauty that raises our souls to the level of forms or universality, so that what is violated is the very satiety we take in loving one beautiful person and not beauty itself. For Kant, the normal ways of reasoning, morally and causally, must both violate each other in order to produce the huge energy of the ultimate synthesis; for Heidegger what is violated is everydayness in the stasis of inauthenticity. Heidegger is perhaps the most articulate in pointing out the troubling aspects of our existence that necessitates our reluctance to be uncovered. Unless we see that it is entirely natural to resist the denuding of truth, the violence of self-revealing seems arbitrary. Furthermore, for Heidegger the inauthentic is basic and original, it provides us with the structure of existence that must be violated in order to transcend it by thinking; hence we can never dismiss the inauthentic as if it consisted of traits solely of the bovine. The essence of inauthenticity, which must always be presupposed, is its concealing: we are by nature reluctant to learn existential truth, without this reluctance there would be no fundamental ontology. If this sounds quixotic, consider the case of the young man in the first sketch: if there were no fear and hence reluctance to reveal his own being afraid, there would be no courage that violates it, and hence no manifestation of the truth about courage.

Supportive as these three great thinkers may be, it is not enough merely to point out precedents. The suggestion is that, in order for metaphysical thinking to transform us, there must be violence; the nature of the transformation is from being real to the truth of being real. The violence that transforms seems dependent on philosophical reasoning itself, taken in its broadest sense, with an emphasis on dialectical language. No matter how many precedents there are, this seems an arcane and subtle point. What is the difference between being real and the truth of being real, such that the latter is enabled only by language-generated violence to the former? To speak of our own being real at all is something of a mystery, since our normal way of speaking seems to require a distinction between the subject and the object; and if I speak about myself I seem to collapse the two, especially if, in objectifying myself I seem to excise the subjectivity from the concept of myself as object. The terms "subject" and "object" are themselves based on the model of the declarative sentence, and hence are linguistic in their origin. It is, therefore, highly suspicious to reify these terms into metaphysical entities; but so powerful is the seduction of the declarative sentence that it is difficult to escape this error altogether. Yet it is not this grammatical hegemony, together with its persuasion to the metaphysically improper reifications, that accounts for the mystery and hence the violence.

Truth is distinct both from knowledge and the real. There are many things that are true that we do not know, and the truth of something is not the same as the factual existence or metaphysical reality of it, for the table being set is not the same as the truth of the table being set, nor is the reality of my being guilty the same as the truth of my guilt. Yet neither is truth the mere link between knowledge and what is real, though such linkage is in part provided by truth, as when we speak of the discovery of the table being set or the discovery of what it means to be guilty; in these cases discovery is a characteristic of truth as a phenomenon. Whatever is known must first be true, and the real is the ground or basis of truth; but these remarks merely show the interdependence of the notions; they do not suggest and cannot imply reduction of one term to another. Even this interdependence, however, is troubling; for one might ask what is the sense of truth mattering unless I know it, or what else is reality except that which, as known, would be true? Truth does matter independently of knowledge, and reality may be the ground of truth but cannot of itself provide it. These warnings are not idle; it is far too easy to lose the autonomous worth and meaning of truth altogether in our concern for the more intuitively obvious and more easily identifiable notions of knowledge and the real.

More troubling is the possible role that language may play in our understanding of knowledge, truth, and reality. Perhaps truth is, as is suggested by Bertrand Russell, only in propositions. Even as this suggestion fades as indefensible, the thinker most dramatically opposed to Russell, Martin Heidegger, also suggests that language—though not as propositional, to be sure—is a fundamental resource for truth. The reason for this appeal to language by both thinkers is that if reality and knowledge are themselves inadequate to truth, perhaps the linkage between them, language, may suffice. Even if the introduction of language is helpful, however, it is not sufficient; not all language is truthful, and not all senses of truth need verbal articulation.

The phenomena must be analyzed directly. We might say the fact that the table is set is true when its being set is manifested to us, so that truth is not merely the reality of the table being set but is its manifestation. What, though, is manifest? Is it the simple fact, or is it the richly variant levels of meaning? Even if manifestation is more broadly conceived than its mere occurrence, in what way is manifestation other than simply being seen or known? Perhaps the truth of the table being set is the revelation and discovery of all that is entailed: we see a finely presented table and discover what it means: we do not eat our food off the ground or with our fingers; the table being set manifests our civility and elegance, so that by its manifestation we not only discover that it is set but learn what it means for it to be set. Is there yet, however, any violence in this? Perhaps not.

I may know I am guilty. As the guilt manifests itself, however, the darker implications of my act, the outrage and pain of my victim, and most important, the dread burden of its self-disclosure on me, are learned in stages of self-discovery. This learning, which may require certain passages of time or levels of self-censure not immediately available at the moment of my guilty act, is a species of manifestation. We often use such vernacular phrases as "the truth dawned on me" in phenomena of this kind. It is not that I am merely adding items of factual information; rather this truth of my guilt "dawning" on me is the revelation or manifestation of what intrudes violently upon my reluctance to accept it, forcing me to endure what I would prefer to keep unrevealed. In such cases to suggest that violence is necessary in the learning of truth seems justified.

Guilt, however, is in itself, always a burden and hence resisted. But the violence of metaphysical learning need not be reluctant: there is a violence in joy or wonder—although now it is perhaps more enlightened to say that the violence is in the learning of joy's truth—just as there is violence in the learning of guilt's truth. Joy's truth is violent in the sense it overwhelms; indeed in its more sublime moments, we are its captive; we speak of being rapt or in ecstasy—being violently ripped out of our previous state. Is this, however, the proper terminology? Is it not joy itself and not joy's "truth" that renders such violence? Joy as a passion may indeed be violent, but the truth of joy as a self-revealing phenomenon may also transform us violently; indeed as a mere passion the moment of joyous feeling may be fleeting, but its truth may abide to the point of being transformed by it. When I speak here of joy's truth I do not mean the realization that I am joyous; rather I speak of learning what it means to be joyous. What it means to be joyous is learned, and this learning has a transforming mentor—it is violent.

In each of the five sketches there is a violent learning that, because of its violence, transforms. What demands attention now can be delayed no longer; we *must* ask: what is the nature of truth such that it can violate?

FIVE

Truth

The friends lay upon their youthful hill beneath the spangled firmament. "How vast the world is! Watching the stars reminds us how puny and insignificant we are. It puts all our petty worries in perspective, doesn't it?" The other nodded, and a long, friendly silence trailed before he spoke. "Yet, here we are, thinking about the vastness, and that just makes *us* matter somehow, maybe even more than the greatness of the expanse itself." His companion smiled, unseen in the dark. "And we can think about ourselves, too, can't we? The night gives us that, making us both insignificant and important at the same time. It's kind of eerie, isn't it?" Then he added with a frought chuckle, "I'm not sure we should stay out here too long."

Something happens to the two friends lying on the hill beneath the stars. What happens—or perhaps better, what begins to happen—is a transformation that is threefold: The first discovery is that truth matters—a phenomenon that is not to be confused with someone taking an interest in something, hence the locution 'truth matters to me' is retrograde and misleading. The next is that truth happens—which must not be understood as knowledge, but as an event that alters us. The third is that truth enables— not merely reveals—meaning: our own being real is rendered thinkable by truth: we can think about what it *means* to be real. Here 'think' cannot be mere opinion, or the entertainment of imaginary possibilities, for there is authority in thinking; nor should it be conceived as a purely mental activity, for truth does not consist of the *result* of such thinking but as the *enablement* of it, perhaps even the violent demand of it. The most challenging task is to confront the now-inevitable question: if we can think with authority (universally) about meaning, what then does meaning itself mean? The suggestion here is that meaning is our own being real in the world established by the transforming violence of truth happening to us. To suggest this, however, regardless of the huge effort it takes to realize it, threatens merely to render the analysis internally consistent, and so it is fitting to ask again: what happens to the two friends after their first observation of the sublime reach of indefinite space and their second, interior realization their thinking about it brings? There is a third discovery, lurking almost unnoticed in the reactions; it emerges with supreme demand and promise: we learn, however vaguely, what it means to be and to think about the truth inherent in both discoveries. It may at first seem that the three stages that occur to the young stargazers can be accounted for by simple shifts in topics or interests. If the currency of a more thoughtful and less hurried exchequer is spent, however, the purchase of their dialectic yields a far richer investment. What happens, we ask, when thinking about the vastness of the expanse makes possible the new realization that it is not the sky alone that stuns, but what enables us to think about it; which then reveals the truth of our own awesome reality? Not only is our thinking transformed, but we ourselves are, too, and so is the world we live in. It is indeed eerie. It is not the vastness that is eerie; it is the self-discovery that brings with it a certain unease. Who are we to think about the universe? Who are we to think about—and feel—what it *means* to think about the universe? Whatever else we realize, the ineluctable discovery is that we are in the vast universe, and being in it changes fundamentally what the universe must be. A carrot, also being in the universe, makes up a tiny part of it, too; but there's nothing in a carrot that fundamentally changes the very meaning of the world. A thinker able to think of the whole world, including his own thinking of it, demands an entire reevaluation of what reality means. It is not only we who are transformed but the universe itself, for now the universe can be the object of our thought, and must be thought of as being able to contain thinkers capable of grasping its truth.

Recent discoveries in astronomy are surely thrilling, for the advancement of our knowledge about the great cosmological questions cannot be dismissed as trivial. Yet, in some ways there is fog in this erudition: that there may be life elsewhere cannot outrank the importance that there is life here. What is visible in the vault of a starry night, we now are told, are celestial objects of such magnitude they are almost all necessarily conceived as mere gargantuan blobs of gaseous matter, undergoing huge nuclear explosions generating the energy that allows them to be seen over galactic distances. If there is life elsewhere, it is on the smaller moons or planets invisible to us: we can, with our naked eyes see only some of our own planets and distant suns, apparently like our own sol, erupting nuclear fireballs. We have sent space probes to the planets of our solar system, and thus far the evidence is fairly bleak: they are merely big rocks or gaseous bubbles. The magnitude of them, in both size and numbers, dwarfs our earth to such puny rank we seem to let our pettiness of size suggest a pettiness of worth and being. There are no beings on the faces of the millions of nuclear suns who lie upon their green hills and wonder about the universe. Furthermore, if gazing at the stars seem to put our concerns into a perspective that makes them trivial, a great disservice is wrought on truth. The billions of celestial objects in no way can trivialize our guilt if we have wronged a friend or hurt a child or demeaned ourselves: that we can murder, steal, rape, betray, and vulgarize is not rendered less terrible by the terrible vastness of celestial eruptions. Indeed, gazing at the stars provokes our wonder; and it is our wonder that matters, not only the stars. To the young friends lying on our local hill, the discovery of the self within the world is but a glimpse or insight; this glimpse may serve as a spark to ignite the fuse of thought. Many lie upon hills and feel moved by a profound truth, but if discarded as a passing thrill, akin to a daunting ride at an amusement park, it is not wonder but simple visceral delight in the vertiginous. We must think about our thinking.

The transformation, however, is nevertheless enabled by the moment. Can there be a world without our thinking it? There certainly could be a vast multitude of entities if there were no thinking, but the term "world" provides a coherence that comes only when thought. It is the second shift that then matters: the thinker is not merely another item in the world, but the one who provides the coherence, not only among the multitudinous galaxies but between them and our thoughtful being in the world. That I am a tiny speck on an already tiny planet means—what? How am I to think about such phenomena? Why should the measure of my reality and my truth be gauged solely by the physical size of anything? Taken from the opposite perspective of a nuclear physicist studying the makeup of atoms and quarks, I am gigantic. Perhaps what amazes in both sciences is not the sizes but the laws: what does it mean for there to be laws governing both galaxies and quarks such that they are orderly and hence can be thought about? Since we are the only ones we yet know who think about such laws, our comprehension of them renders us unique in this sense: whatever enables me to calculate external phenomena cannot be the same as that which enables me to think about what it means to calculate them.

There is in this discovery a danger: the term "thinking" must not be so narrowly conceived as to omit the feeling of wonder and awe. It is not only that I can somehow figure out how big those galactic reaches are, but that I can palpably sense their enormity and even my own belonging and alienation. This can be analyzed more deeply by realizing that what adds to our wonder is the sheer indifference of the natural: it is not only the size of the external universe that seems to belittle us, but its mechanistic inevitability, we sense the universe as alien because it grinds on mercilessly with no restraints or moral anchors, as if it were an impersonal machine ultimately crushing us with its unfeeling power. Such a world literally could have no room at all for beings who care and matter; and so we tend to disjoin the world from its people. Somehow, as morally and existentially significant, we seem not to belong to such a world, nor it to us. It is then too easy to suggest the indifferent cosmos of relentless matter and energy is alone real, whereas we who care and wonder are somehow not real; only the atoms that make up our spatial extension are real, for they too are mechanistic. Yet the temptation to take refuge in this metaphysical disjunction is resistible, even demanded. Nature is remorseless, but it is not the world. How then are we to think of the world as including nature but not reduced to it? Merely to suggest that in addition to nature there are in the world non-natural entities called people will not suffice, for such a suggestion ineptly states the problem, not the solution. It is an inept statement of the problem because it is in thrall of naturalist diction: 'nonnatural entities' inevitably uses the natural entity as the paradigm, both in the noun and adjective; but the real is paradigmatically neither natural nor made up of entities. There is no escaping the realization that our being in the world is itself a problem inherent in what it means to be in the world: we in the world—rather than we and the world—requires thought. To come to grips with this problem transforms: we, in the world, are a problem. The young stargazers on the hill briefly sense this: it is an eerie realization, but one that cannot be dismissed without losing something precious: that truth matters. That truth matters must transform what is meant by 'world,' and by 'us.'

Cognition is not the premier access to the truth of the world; we are not primarily knowers of the world; we abide in it, belong in it, find our existential ground in it, and learn in it. To ask what it means to gaze at the stars is to confront the world as strange and familiar, local and foreign, welcoming and rejecting. If the vast indifference of hostile places alienates by its naturalistic intransigence, their distance is a comfort, for we are welcome just because the world as near also offers a place to dwell, and dwelling is enabled by reality; and as real, truth is grounded in it.

Something, we say, *happens* to the two young friends lying on the hill. What happens to them? Perhaps so many things happen that no single answer suffices: they are compelled to think; they are made to seem small, then large; they are, however briefly, ripped out of commonality and confronted with the extraordinary; they discover, though yet do not understand, their own linkage to the world and the world to them; they are made uneasy, yet uplifted; they may even feel denuded in a way, as if some inner secret were exposed. Yet the profligacy of these events occurs not as discrete and distinct, but somehow as one; and the only term that unifies them as a single notion is truth. The locution may sound odd: truth, we suggest, happens to them. It is not only truth as a necessary but not sufficient condition of knowledge; it is also truth as a lure, truth as a phenomenon, truth as grounded in reality. What happens to them is truth as grounded in their reality, but above all truth that enables—and sometimes enables so forcefully as to require—them to confront what it means for them to be real. What happens to them is the violence of truth enabling them to *be* meaningful *because of* truth, and they are meaningful because they can, with authority, think about what it means for them to be who they are in the world. What it means for them to be in the world is forced upon them as thinkable; paradoxically the world is revealed as being enabled as world only by thought, even as thought as thought is enabled by their being in the world. This thinkability of the world as ours and us as already in the world is sui generis: it is not science nor art, not logic nor moral judging. It is philosophy. The temptation—and it is a powerful seduction that must be resisted—is to see it as mere reflection, or as "second order knowledge." Though it be sui generis, it is not, however, entirely unfamiliar. No one word may be entirely adequate, but since the discovery seems to confront what it means to be who we are in the world, and what the world means with us being in it, perhaps to think about meaning is to become transformed into truth—not only "the truth about" such things as happen in the world, but being as truth.

It is now necessary to move the two young friends briefly from the pleasant, nightly hill to a hill overlooking a vast carnage wrought by war. This too is not only confronted but self-confronted. Who are we that can do such horrible things? One might look upon the ravaged hosts and first proclaim fierce outrage: this ought not to have happened! But as the consideration deepens, an even darker revulsion may occur: is this *our* work? Then I no longer can take any delight in, or have any affection for, my own kind. It is better to be a rock or a carrot, for the shame is unendurable. This is our truth: misanthropy. To think about the meaning of our existence entails the ineluctable truth that seems not only to cancel worth but positively assails it: it is far better not to be than to be.

This may well be a hurried judgment, but its impact is not to be slighted. There is no guarantee that what we find in metaphysical discovery will conform to our esteem; we are only guaranteed that such learning transforms. It may take considerable labor to persist in self-learning to realize that even horrors are true, and as true carry with them the worth of inquiry. Yet as they look upon the Asian magnitude of the slaughtered, one might recall a Lincoln at Gettysburg: that these dead have not died in vain; that they who lie here have given the last full measure of devotion. Were these slain willing to take the risks? Did some die nobly, knowing of their sacrifice? Perhaps such courage and devotion recasts the field of death in such a way that honor and not only revulsion sweeps across the field of thought. Just as the stars render us small yet great because we think on them, so the sacrificed dead fill us with both smallness and greatness in our truth. Is it really more astonishing that men should slaughter men in vast numbers, than that men should risk such slaughter because the fields of blood are dearly theirs, and their belonging matters, even beyond life? How can we even make such judgments? Yet we cannot escape: judge we must. The dead, no less than the stars, await our enforced thinking: truth again matters—not merely "to us" but as absolute; i.e., it makes a difference in the world—and we cannot escape its demand, but we can deceive ourselves in insouciance. We are transformed by compulsion to recognize these problems as ours, that to turn away from them unconsidered is shameful, yet to confront them is dreadful and difficult.

We do, legitimately, make judgments of terrible dimensions; the compulsion is not to put an end to the terror of these realizations, but to confront them. We can be aware of the horrors of war even as we are aware of the stunning nobility of sacrifice. The question here is not yet which is the proper assessment, but rather what it means to *judge* our being in the world at all. If we do not judge it, or if we try to benumb ourselves into a coma of nonasking, we then become ignoble ourselves. There is violence in this duty: who are we to judge? Answer: we are those who must judge. And from whence comes this unasked and unwanted authority? Truth. Truth, then, does not merely *enable* such judging, but demands it. It is demanded of us even when lying youthfully upon hills beneath stars. We are in the world; and being in it changes what the world means because it is only we who think the world *as* world. But the shift from hill to hill raises a new question: how can truth be the enablement of both the wonder at the stars and the revulsion, coupled with our awe at courage and sacrifice, at the battlefield? Is not the first wonder entirely distinct from the second? It may be different, but not entirely distinct, for in both cases who we are is forced upon us in such a way as to demand we think about what it means to be who we are. Yet the difference is so impressive it cannot be dismissed. If we bring the young friends back to the original hill, we may imagine the further discourse.

"Do you think there are other planets out there with people on them? Maybe not exactly like us, but close enough so that we could think of them as being amazed by the stars?"

"Well, given the vast number of stars and planets, and the immense periods of time that have elapsed from what scientists tell us is the likely start of our universe, I guess the odds of our being the only thinkers is quite small."

"Yes, I've heard that estimate. I'm not sure we are the only thinking beings; I just don't know. There may be others. But your argument is disturbing. You speak about odds. But such estimations of probability rest on the assumption that our own existence here on earth is due entirely to what you call 'odds.' It is not obvious to me that we are the result of chance, or 'odds,' for that is to say we are explainable merely by nature. Nature is, I believe, in part, evolutionary: given enough time and diversity of primal energy I suppose it is inevitable that certain atoms or forces of energy would collect into carbon, nitrogen, oxygen, and hydrogen in such a way as to produce the first reproductive organism; and once you have that, evolution in biology might produce advanced animal species. This would explain us as the result of probabilities; and if that does explain us, then, and only then, can you argue that the *odds* are that there are other people on other planets. Is that what you mean?

"That's what I would have to mean, isn't it? I'm not sure I do mean that, though. I'm uneasy with it."

"What makes you uneasy?"

"I'm not sure. As you pointed out, to think that way necessitates that everything we do—art, sacrifice, reason, love, and even wonder—is simply a natural event, explainable by the same principles that explain other natural events. Either nature is much more than we thought—in which case I'm not sure it should be called 'nature' anymore—or there is in the world truth that is not explained by nature. I didn't realize that talking about the odds that there are other people in the universe naturally rendered me an evolutionary naturalist. I wish I hadn't made the suggestion."

"I'm glad you did. It shows that looking at the stars is more awesome than . . . looking at the stars."

"So maybe all these glittering spots are merely gaseous bubbles or rocks; so I shouldn't feel so small."

"Not all the rocks in the world are worth as much as one person."

"Yes. Well. But rocks and bubbles are real, just as real as people, aren't they?"

"Maybe. But to say we and rocks are equally real is to deny our worth is real, so judgments of worth are merely what we deem them to be, not what they are in reality. If worth is not based in reality, then judgments of worth can't be *true*."

"You keep doing that! You keep pointing out hidden presuppositions in what seems the most obvious claims in the world, and these presuppositions are untenable. Are you saying we are more real than the stars? That sounds silly."

"Well, if you have worth and the rock doesn't—it only has circumstantial value—and if worth is true, what grounds it as true is reality; so you have either 'more' reality than rocks, or a higher degree of reality than rocks."

"Why not simply say there are two different realities, the stars and us? Hold it! Even I can see that won't do. There can be two or three or even more kinds of *things* in the world, but there can't be two worlds or two realities. But why would you say we are more real than rocks?"

"Because, as I just said, judgments of worth can be true, and the true is grounded in the real. Are you suggesting there is not truth in judgments of worth?"

"If there were no truth in worth, I would have to be a moral and aesthetic relativist, and since I know it is wrong to torture someone merely to please myself, I cannot adopt such a position. So, yes, there is truth is judging worth, and just saying that makes me tremble all over in both dread and eagerness, for with you and the stars to poke me, I'm in for a mighty struggle and I wish to hell we hadn't come out here, but I guess I'm kind of glad we did. In spite of your arguments, though, I still resist the idea that reality permits of degrees. Something either is or it isn't."

"That I support. Given any entity—and that's what I take you to mean by the word *something*—it either exists or does not. We ask whether, and we answer that. We ask whether ghosts exist, and we answer that they do not. However, our questions are not limited to 'whether,' they also include 'what,' so I can distinguish whether we exist—yes, we do—from what we are—what it means to be real can be thought about *as true*."

"And I take it you're suggesting that what it means to be real includes in some sense a consideration of our worth. Since we can be more or less worthy, you therefore want to say we can be more or less real."

"Unless worth and reality are linked, I don't see how any judgment made about our worth can be true. However, since that is all I demand, perhaps I am wrong about reality permitting of degrees. It's still true, though, that what it means for us to be real is worthier than what it means for rocks to be real—though actually all I know is that rocks exist; I'm not sure I do know their essence. Rather, it seems I should say that what it means for a rock to be real is for it to be seen and confronted by us as obdurate entities outside ourselves. If you will grant that much, I'll drop all reference to degrees of reality."

"Well, we might drop it, or at least suspend it. After all, my first reaction when we came out here was how small and puny the stars made me feel, and that is a feeling about worth, isn't it? What you've done is to show such worth is not merely felt, but thought—that is, it's part of truth. But if truth is necessarily grounded in reality, then perhaps we ought to entertain the notion that real permits of degrees, especially if we can ask about the meaning of being real. Why did you back off so readily? If what you think might be true, you can't be indifferent to it."

"Well, we *can* be indifferent, but we ought not to be. Look, though, what we're doing, right now. We're thinking and giving reasons about the whole world and what it means for us to be thinking about it. We weigh and discard suggestions because they seem incoherent, or we accept them provisionally because they seem to promise greater understanding. Why do our concerns for coherence and understanding in questions about meaning matter? One reason is surely because coherence or thinkability is necessary for truth and inquiry, but another is because what it means to be in the world is to realize that thinking—a part of which is coherence—is essential for truth, and must also be essential for reality: what's real cannot be incoherent. We can ask what reality—or rather, what being real—means. I guess what excites me is that questioning about meaning entails suggestions that might be true; even and especially suggestions about what it means to be real. Isn't that amazing?"

"Aren't *we* amazing? Let's go in."

They had to go in, of course: the stars were dimming. The suggestion that emerges from their talk can be put in the form of a question: why account for truth as enabling judgment and thinking rather than the other way around? Usually truth is seen as the product of thinking or judging, or even a mere relation between thought and thing. But if truth transforms, it cannot be a mere relation, nor can it be embedded in propositions. Is it not more traditional, and indeed sounder, to suggest the following: granted the two friends were transformed; but what transforms them is their own thinking, provoked by the psychological feelings of smallness and awe that come from looking at the stars? It is no different in kind from being transformed from incautious to cautious by the pain of touching a hot stove: I won't do that again. Truth, as enabling, according to this analogy, has nothing to do with it. Accordingly, it is merely the psychological feelings that transform them. But transformation cannot be reduced to mere changes in attitude; it is rather a metaphysical and ultimate recasting of reality itself, and hence truth must be central to it. Because what happens to us is a transformation of our being real—and hence what reality itself means—the violence that can wreak such profound alteration can only be that which enables a similarly profound alteration in our thinking, and only truth can play this dual role. Truth becomes active rather than passive—indeed truth itself is transformed from that which is enabled by thought to that which *enables* thought. Metaphysical truth is therefore always about, even as it enables, meaning; and on its highest level, what is enabled is what it means to be real (and not, as in the ordinary sense of truth, the other way around in which being real enables its truth).

To speak of truth as enabling or demanding may require further reflection. How can truth "demand"? Truth is not a moral precept, nor an officer in the navy, nor a natural law; these three can legitimately be said to demand. How can truth "enable"? Physical causes enables certain events, learned skills enable high performance, the Constitution enables us to speak freely without government reprisal; but truth is neither a cause nor a skill nor a legal document. To understand truth as a metaphysical phenomenon requires that it be seen in terms of its existential totality, and not as a mere relation. 'Being to the south of' is a relation; as such it is a perspective based on a constructed scheme, in this cases a standard map, which allows us to locate New Orleans in relation to Chicago. Truth in the propositional sense is based solely on the *relation* of correspondence, so that what matters is the fact and the proposition that relates to that fact. But relations are not phenomena. To speak of truth as a phenomenon is to recognize its metaphysical status in terms of what it means for truth to be, which includes, but is not restricted to, how individual propositions, as true, are made possible. How are we to think this more clearly? An analogy may be helpful. A response to the question, Why should I not park in the intersection? might be, Because it is against the law. Here the phrase "the law" is richly ambivalent. On the one hand it refers to a specific local ordinance or statute, which can be identified by number and reference. On the other hand, the ordinance or statute itself is only meaningful in terms of "the law" as a phenomenon, which includes such elements as policemen giving tickets, judges in courtrooms, lawyers practicing their craft; it also includes the intimidating if magnificent notions of such things as civilization itself, the universality of rights and duties, the legitimacy of the Constitution, to say nothing of the vast philosophical literature since the ancients on such matters as the origin and meaning of law. These altogether constitute the phenomenon of law. Yet, a mere local ordinance presupposes all these vast and ponderous issues; even as, in some sense, the actual fine or incarceration imposed by actual police officers may be the most concrete and immediate realization of law in praxis. The analogy is this: propositional truth is akin to law as a specific ordinance; the phenomenon of truth is akin to law in the metaphysical sense, meaning law as rooted in the very nature of human existence. The phenomenon of law consists in the various ways we must think about law and how the various levels of law, from theories to constitutions to courtrooms fit together, and not in the mere plurality of individual statutes. The analogy, then, suggests that the phenomenon of truth includes the various universal ways we think about truth, and how truth actually works in all of its variant meanings. How, though, *do* we think about truth beyond that of the traditional theoretical accounts such as correspondence, coherence, and pragmatic relevance? At the onset of this chapter, reflecting on the first brief vingette of the friends on the hills, truth was characterized as (1) mattering (2) happening (3) ennabling (4) revealing and (5) demanding. A brief account of these ascriptions in reverse order may be helpful. What does it mean to say that truth itself, and not merely the psychological persuasion of an interested individual inquirer, *demands*? What does it demand? How does it demand? To whom is the demand made? The last is perhaps most revealing: every rational being who reflects at all is demanded, and in two ways: first, every reflective being as reflective can *be* reflective only because such reflection is not optional: there is a sense that it is somehow dutiful to inquire and shirking not to inquire; second, the nature of inquiry itself is such that reason, evidence, authority, and rational discovery "order" us, almost as a command, to abandon the antithoughtful beliefs, and to continue to seek even if the seeking is difficult. Why this strange locution? Why not say rather that it is in our interest to learn philosophical truth? Interest may not be strong enough. There is authority in a seeking that is propped by argumentation and evidence, an authority that makes its demand on us, not the other way around. Truth demands because of its authority as a phenomenon.

Truth also reveals. This is a Heideggerian argument in some sense, but it obviously has a status independent of, and prior to, his articulation of it.

What truth reveals is meaning or thinkability. At a trial the defendent's guilt can be revealed not by a single testimony or an item of evidence, but by the entire proceeding; yet a great drama, such as Shakespeare's *Richard III* or O'Neil's *The Iceman Cometh* can also reveal what guilt itself means. In such cases, the trial or the play can be said to reveal guilt, and such revelation is a species of discovery that patently belongs to what we mean by the phenomenon of truth. To say truth also enables has its roots in the Kantian critique: we can account for how experience is possible by reflecting on the faculties that must be presupposed in order for cognitive acts to occur. A faculty is that which enables us to do something. Yet, the notion of truth as enabling has for greater significance and application than found in Kantian orthodoxy. In enabling us to be able to reflect on what enables us, we reach the highest level of thought—philosophy—which further enables truth to transform us by its enabling. That is, we are made able to learn our own powers; and this requires the suggestion that it is not our powers than enable truth but rather truth, as a phenomenon, that enables our powers. How else could self-learning be possible?

That truth can be said to happen is required if we are to consider it as a phenomenon. What happens to the friends on the hill is an event, an educational event if you will, in which learning *occurs*. That such learning has the status as an event, and hence can happen, requires that we consider this phenomenon of learning as a part of the broader phenomenon of truth, thereby allowing the provocative locution that truth happens. What happens in the courtroom in which the truth of the defendent's guilt is made manifest or appears is an event, and hence a phenomenon, that is a smaller element in the larger phenomenon of truth happening. What happens to the friends on the hill, however, is not merely one among many possible phenomena but an event that has a status that is fundamental. To suggest that truth happens as a fundamental phenomenon has this enormous metaphysical benefit of providing a locus for truth that has a nobler status than that of a mere relation.

That truth matters may be the most difficult to explain, for the instinctive addendum "to whom?" must be resisted. To say that truth matters *to* someone suggests the possibility it may not matter to someone else. Even if we were to add that truth matters to every rational being, even if many do not realize this or even deny it, is to yield to a personalist attitude of individuals, even if generalized. It is not merely a generality that truth matters, but a universality; hence the personalist addendum "to whom?" is not required. Truth matters, period. What does this mean? It means, in part, the truth has intrinsic worth, which is troubling because of the putative authority of the fact/value distinction. Facts are distinct from values, for values are subjective and facts are objective; but this does not translate to worth and reality, for worth is not subjective and reality is not an object. This echoes what the two friends consider on the second visit to their hill. Worth is real and reality is worthy, though this does not mean every real thing is worthy.

Both notions are meaningful because their opposites are possible. Once we distinguish the subjective notion of value from the universal one of worth, and the metaphysically prior notion of reality from the epistemically grounded fact, the suggestion that truth has worth cannot be dissuaded by appeals to the fact/value distinction. With this clarification it may now be reasonable to accept that truth matters; but in realizing this we are now forced to consider what avails our access to the notion of truth mattering, and we find that it is not, as one might be prone first to accept, knowledge that provides this. Rather, since the present reflection is on truth as an existential phenomenon, we begin to discern that a similar focus must be placed on our ability to discover such truth. Hence we must shift from the traditional focus on knowledge, to the more important phenomenon of learning.

What it means for us to be real cannot be revealed merely by an analysis of our consciousness or mind, and certainly not by a consideration of knowledge. The epistemological approach is simply too narrow. Yet neither should the approach be too broad, for not everything we do is metaphysically significant, and certainly how we think about our daily activities is not metaphysical thinking. Almost everything we do can be rendered profound by poets and thinkers, but in such cases it is how we think about them that makes them worthy of thought, not their topicality. This complicates the matter, for how are we to know in advance how to rank our acts and experiences so that we are not distracted by the banal and the inane? Why should we have to know such ranking in advance? Advance of what? Yet if, in some sense, I do not know in advance what topics are worthy of thought and which are unworthy, then is not the caveat to avoid banality an impediment to the possibility of such avoidance?

It is one of the things we learn. We learn to discriminate between the worthy and the unworthy, the banal and the profound; indeed we even learn how to learn such judgments. What, then, does it mean to learn in such a way so that we learn about what it means to be real? What does it mean to learn to be transformed by truth? A new paradox seems to emerge. If we are to learn about our own being real, then it seems we must learn only what we have already learned. If my own being real is available to me directly, then it would seem I could not possibly study what it means to be real because I already am real. In one sense we do indeed learn what we have learned. In the following chapter, an actual historical figure will be studied as a paradigm of how we learn what we already are.

SIX

The Learner

They gave the last full measure of devotion, he told us; and by doing so they enabled their country, based on liberty and equality eighty-seven years earlier, to triumph over insurrection. Even today this great battlefield address sends trickles of thrill along the spine. It is a masterpiece of oratory, perhaps even of poetry. There is great beauty and great truth in it. It helped transform a war, a history, a people—even the world. The study of it may even help transform us as learners of our heritage and of the truth inherent in it. Rich and productive though such considerations may be, however, the focus of the present inquiry is not on how we may learn from the address, but how its author was transformed by his own learning of his and our own reality to enable it. Insofar as the speech at Gettysburg is a poetic artwork, it is the result of genius, and is thus beyond explanation, for genius does not follow rules of aesthetic coherence but provides them. However, insofar as the speech also reflects the wisdom learned by a great student, perhaps by marking the stages of his erudition we can reveal concretely how and why tranformational, metaphysical learning not only must take place in a rich culture, but must also rely on its inheritance. Since genuine learning is always of the true, it cannot be culturally relative; but the profundity of this learning is impossible to obtain without the enabling provided by a specific, historical tradition. It is thus possible to track the violent, eruditional wisdom of Lincoln as it transformed him into one of the greatest learners in human history.

The America in which Lincoln grew up as a farm boy, laborer, and then local lawyer, was a vast political patchwork of deceits; to use a modern psychological term, Americans were in a state of denial. In 1776, the slaveholding Thomas Jefferson had written that all men are created equal, and this irony had developed into a fundamental rift that could not last much longer without bold resolution. There were slave dealers, slaveholders, abolitionists, emancipators, anti-Union Northerners and pro-Union Southerners, indifferentists, fanatics, and those who were so confused they simply stopped thinking about it. Congress was by far the strongest branch of government, the presidency had been greatly weakened; in the Senate were some brilliantly skilled manipulators who offered compromise after compromise to keep the two institutions, Union and slavery, intact. Men such as Clay, Webster, Calhoun, and Douglas were balancing the spinning plates of tactical maneuvers on long political poles, like clowns in a circus. Western expansion, huge immigrations from Ireland and continental Europe, and the Industrial Revolution were stretching the fabric of society beyond these senatorial patches. We should not forget that most of the Western civilized world accepted slavery when the nineteenth century began; within a single lifetime of sixty years, most of that world had rejected it. In America, however, the "peculiar institution" had curious rootage in the South that was more sociological and racial than economic; so that even the Tsar of autocratic Russia eliminated serfdom before the freedom-loving Americans could rid themselves of slaves. The almost tragic trust Americans had in the Senate to pull off continuing political compromises exacerbated this odd blindness to the inherent contradictions in the political arena. Lincoln himself, in the 1840s and 1850s seemed to echo this self-deceit: he hated slavery, he saw that a house divided against itself could not stand, yet he rejected abolition, and even supported, on political grounds, continuation of the peculiar institution in states that included it in their own laws. As were most of his contemporaries, he was not yet a racial egalitarian, for he insisted at one point that as a white male he was superior to a black female. Clearly, his own thinking on the great issues was not yet fully developed; or to put it another way, his famed honesty now had to be directed at himself. He needed, then, to think more deeply on the matter, for he sensed that the directionless muddle both in his own mind and in the nation as a whole was itself contributing to the drift toward crisis. He therefore launched an unparalleled curriculum on himself, designed to uncover the truth of his—and our—own being real. This learning can be divided into two distinct "classrooms": the first was akin to a lecture, the second a tutorial. Much of the former took place prior to his presidency, much of the latter as Commander in Chief; yet they belong together in a single cruel academy of metaphysical self-learning. Worse, he also sensed that these political compromises were distorting truth: they blinded us to our own reality.

THE FIRST CLASSROOM

What is remarkable about the first classroom were its teachers: a pair of documents—the Declaration of Independence and the federal Constitution. As the political crisis deepened, so did the metaphysical confusion about our reality. To be adled about the very essence of one's being requires deep thought to extricate it. The more fiery speculators and political patchers of his day would make up "doctrines" with opportunistic labels, especially Stephen Douglas who, in support of the Kansas-Nebraska Act of 1854, maintained the ad hoc principle of squatter sovereignty that sounded so appealing to the populist belief in majority rule. This act, more than any other, unleashed the final political forces that would lead to war. Lincoln was thus obliged to return to the two enabling documents; but not as mere supports to his political understanding of the Union, rather as the ground for his own, deeper penetration into our being real. He sensed the original wisdom either had been forgotten—or perhaps more likely—had never come to full fruition. He began to toil in the hard bedrock of these documents, not merely as political guides, or even contracts; rather they were enablers of a way of thinking—American thinking that made possible the reality of the nation. Lincoln left no written account of his reflections, no diary or manifesto of his development as thinker; though he provided hints of his discovery in speeches and letters. It is nevertheless possible to think through what these steps must have been, and to engage him with our own reflections on the documents. What follows, therefore, is not discovered by mere historical research, though it is certainly consistent with the documents themselves and with Lincoln's actions and public declarations. Another way to put it is to point out we also have the same founding documents as Lincoln had; and *we* can dig into them and learn from them, and be guided in our learning by what we do know about Lincoln and his time. It is helpful to focus on four passages, two from each document, and reflect on how Lincoln learned the truth they contained by thinking *metaphysically* about them.

1. "We hold these Truths to be self-evident, that all Men are created equal, that they are endowed by their Creator with certain unalienable Rights . . ." This first part of the sentence that begins the second paragraph of the Declaration is not merely an historic, political claim that helps to justify the Colonies' break from England; nor is it a blindly accepted first principle in a logical proof. It is instructive as well as establishing, and by its own language invites deeper thought. A product of the rationalistic Enlightenment, it nevertheless enables its readers to realize the fundamental trust in human reason, and the absolute authority of truth. These twenty-four words inevitably link rights to thinking and thinking to rights. For Lincoln, and for us following his reading, the point of this connection was in need of exposure just because in his day it seemed to be overlooked. To be able to think is the ultimate origin of rights that could not be denied. To concretize this, it is helpful to consider Lincoln's point in claiming his "superiority" both as white and male over the black female. Her inferiority, even if accepted, could not eradicate the truth of her humanity. In an almost Kantian manner, with the help of the Declaration, he recognized the black female was yet a person. As

a person, she was able to think, and because she could think, she too could discover the self-evident truths that included liberty. Because she could *think* these truths, she had the rights. The connection is often overlooked: these truths, the Declaration stated, were self-evident; this does not mean they are glibly obvious or even intuitive; rather it means that any thinker can figure them out by thinking seriously on them—that is: they are learnable. One need not have a particular bloodline, or have a specific education at higher schools, or have a certain social status or color of skin; one need not even be born in any particular spot; if they were inherent in the nature of reason itself, however deeply buried, as reasoner the discoverer of these truths was enabled by their discovery to the right itself. The phrase "among these rights" suggests there are others than those listed; but it also implies that our access to them rests upon our common ability to think. The close inferential connection between the notion of self-evident truths and the rights that are unalienable (later spelled "inalienable")—that is, rights that follow from our rational nature and hence cannot be alienated or taken away—is itself the result of the thinking on truth that establishes the right. Many historians have pointed out that Lincoln had reestablished the Declaration as the more fundamental of the two founding documents. How did he arrive at this? The Constitution includes in itself the right to amend; indeed this provision is one of the most precious and successful of its offerings, making it a living, changing, and developing organ of the body politic. But one does not amend self-evident truths. What is said in the Declaration cannot be changed or amended, though its language admits incompleteness as to the listing of rights. In the formal sense, then, the Declaration is about the fundamental truths and the rights that follow from their being discerned by all who think.

Every right requires thought, not only as its basis, but as to its reality—that is, its meaning. The very first listed is that we are all equal. Since not all are equal in the qualities or natural virtues, the claim seems tepid; for vast differences in intelligence, creativity, wealth, ingenuity, physical health and beauty, as well as just plain luck, surely make a mockery of claims about undifferentiated equality. The right, when considered thoughtfully, however, is not that impotent: it clearly means equality before the law. Each citizen has the same protection and status, regardless of personal or human inequality. The mother country, England, recognized lords and commoners; others recognized aristocrats as legally privileged over the common workers; the rule of primogeniture was long established throughout Europe. But if the rights of citizens—indeed the rights of all who are able to think self-evident truth—are equal just because the truth *is* available, even though it may not always be obvious or recognized, then the autonomous worth of each person and the autonomous worth of the law based on thinking or reasoning were interconnected. It is thus not equality that gives law its universality, but the other way around; it is the universality of law as law that grounds legal equality. What may trouble is how Jefferson and Lincoln both could support a nation that allowed slavery in some of its states. Were these men egalitarian in their reason but elitist in their actions? At least Lincoln did not own slaves, but he was not yet ready to abolish the institution. Were the claims in the Declaration, then, mere ideals? Were they distant goals, perhaps never to be achieved in mortal life? Even worse: were they utopian? To us in the twenty-first century it may seem these famed figures were unprincipled in their behavior: they spoke fine words but did not follow the dictates of their minds. If Lincoln was able to see the connection between self-evident truth and the rights to be thought of and treated accordingly, he was also able to recognize that perfection is often the enemy of what can be achieved. He also knew the document does not end with the statement of truth providing rights, but continues:

2. "—That to secure these Rights, Governments are instituted among Men, deriving their just Powers from the Consent of the Governed . . ." This passage, too, is in need of clarification: what does "consent of the governed" mean? It certainly cannot mean that each citizen must agree with each law, for that is anarchy, not government. Yet, neither can it mean simply the rule of the majority; for if we have "unalienable" rights even the majority cannot take them away. Vague phrases such as "the will of the people" or "the common good" were dangerous in their inexactitude, so ephemeral they could be and were used elsewhere to support a dictator. Lincoln did not have to speculate abstractly about this, for there was solid evidence that the already established and ongoing Constitution was indeed effective just because, as a republic in which every citizen could vote, and voters could be impaneled on juries, there was indeed consent. About him and around him were forces at work, concrete and palpable, useful and authoritative, that manifested consent: even small town councils, dogcatchers, postal officers—Lincoln's own job for a brief period—state senators, sheriffs, governors, were all elected; on the circuit were cases brought before juries, made up of twelve men from the community. Sometime Lincoln won his cases, sometimes he lost; more important, sometimes the *government* lost. This was consent in action, grounded in the rule of law. What is of importance for this inquiry is the connection between the documental and the concrete. In his daily life, Lincoln and most other Americans absorbed the existential phenomenon of America's reality as it manifested itself; but when political discord seemed to stretch and distort along partisan fault lines, he sought for the anchor in truth itself. For him the words of the document were not theoretic or abstract; rather they provided, with the clarity of articulated rules, the guide for thinking. Yet the Declaration claimed the principle of consent was self-evident. The first two words of the quote "We hold" are thus disturbing. Why not simply say, these truths are self-evident? To preface this metaphysical absolute with local identities seems akin to saying "It is merely my opinion that two plus two is four." Suppose

one were to object that since only the Americans "hold" the truths, they are nonuniversal. The claim seems to be about the pronoun, "We, Americans," not the universality of the truth. Such objections are misreadings: the truths are universal, but they are *held* by us; that is, we are their protectors, their embodiments, their voicings to the world: who we are is reflected in our defense of them. To say Lincoln "learned" from the Declaration that government is based on consent does not mean he discovered that it was true because it was written; rather, in thinking about it, he recognized the universality of the "American" truth as grounded in self-evidence or "thinkability." It was not merely formally self-evident, it was also "self-evident" in the developing of the young nation—that is: it was *learnable*. This is metaphysical self-learning, coupling the documents with the actual nation: as thinkers, that we are the origin of our liberties is a metaphysical truth; as Americans such thinking must entail consent, and with this consent the actualization of liberty.

Such thinking and such consenting are not idle. We not only have rights because of our thinking, we also have duties; and Lincoln felt the burden of this duty. His famous remark that he would rather live in Russia where freedom was overtly denied than in a self-deluding democracy in which freedom was proclaimed verbally but denied in reality, reveals his concern: hypocrisy is leprous contagion because it deceives on the ground level of truth, ourselves. If thinking on truth enables rights, antithinking, such as hypocrisy and confusion, thwarts them. To have access to self-evident truth burdens us not only with the need to think, but, if one had leadership gifts, with the duty to reveal and guide. The hypocrisy itself was all the more insidious for being concealed; as the public clamor for liberty grew louder, the achievement of it was diminished. Lincoln was not a speculative thinker, abstractly considering schemes; but he knew that language could serve both as persuader and as truth enabling. The eloquent Douglas persuaded many that the core of American thought was to "let the people decide," so that whether Kansas should be free or slave was up to the people who lived there. Lincoln was learning that such a reading was not only dangerous, it was *false*. His own oratory was designed to let the truth emerge: that consent of the governed was based on laws rooted in self-evident truths; that federal laws could not be based on the consent of people in Kansas but on the consent of the entire Union as unified under law. To break up the Union was to disenable the consent established as true in the Declaration. Lincoln was learning a harsh lesson: the nature of his own oratory had to persuade on the basis of it being learned as true. Hence we see his speeches becoming, more and more, appeals to his listeners' appreciation of clarity and the hard, moral logic inevitable in their origins. This attempt to show the inconsistencies in his opponents and the universality of his own developing wisdom seems at first hearing almost pedantic, so rigorous were his analyses. Yet, this rigor was taking on the slender eloquence of a new, uniquely American, style. The bombast of the great senatorial orations was being replaced with cool, rapierlike analysis that had poetic simplicity. The rich inheritance of the English language cannot be shunned as irrelevant in the education of this backwoods lawyer from Illinois; yet even here can be discerned the dire urgency that drove him to learn as a duty.

3. "We the People . . ." The opening three words of the Preamble to the federal Constitution provoke the need for continuing, ongoing reflection about their meaning. Who were "We, the People"?

A foreign ambassador and an ordinary businessman from Europe were rational beings, and as such were people, and had inherent, reason-based rights. In addition, as visitors to our shores, they were protected by the same laws that governed American citizens. They, however, as noncitizens were not part of the spiritual reality inherent in the "People" of the United States. Therefore, something more than the mere legal protections of the government and the natural rights inherent in being able to think must be presupposed. What do we as Americans enjoy that are not to be found in our visitors? There are, of course, a few formal answers: if they were male, and old enough, and not slaves, they could vote, and as voters, could run for office. Their numbers provided the allotment of seats in Congress; their offspring were also citizens, and if they were born here they could even run for the office of president. But these few legal endowments were relatively minor compared to the more important membership in the national family: it meant something to be American. This spirit, far more elusive to capture than the inheritance of rights, constituted an essential contribution to Lincoln's erudition. How are we to understand it? Were "We the People" simply a political alliance, or act, by which the various sovereign states brought themselves together? Perhaps in 1787 such minimalist understanding could be attributed to the Constitution, but by 1860, Lincoln had an almost mystical or religious reverence for what he called the Union. It was, he reasoned, more akin to a sacrament than to a contract. Just as matrimony makes sacred a union of two unrelated adults, from which an entirely new family develops, so the Union brought us together as a familial people. This spirit of sacramentality marks a development impossible for the eighteenth century rationalism that had helped found the federal government. The Enlightenment had contributed nobly by its focus on reason, and the notion of self-evident truths was consistent with this rationalist rejection of emotive and uncritical beliefs. But the nineteenth century idealists, initiated by Kant, found the extremes of rationalism to be retrograde to the full development of the human person. Passion was reinserted into the search for wisdom, and the purely formal accounts of the operations of the mind were found to be inadequate to account for spirit. Lincoln learned that the nation was not only logically based; it was also a spiritual reality. If the Constitution was invoked by "We the People," then the spiritual or even sacramental quality of that living organism had to be recognized and learned. Yet, this spirit was still based on truth, made available by our receptive and authoritative consciousness; indeed one could still appeal to "reason," as long as one accepted a broader understanding of that term. The American spirit was still rooted in the two founding documents; the centrality of truth in the Declaration was of fundamental importance: Lincoln was forced to learn that truth.

4. "In Order to form a more perfect Union . . ." To understand the dilemma facing both Lincoln and the nation it is necessary to see the tensions that were at work, and still are at work, between law and liberty. We all realize, perhaps vaguely, that liberty is impossible without law; and that law, rather than mere power, is impossible without liberty. How, though, do we synthesize them; how to bring them together? How should we *think* them together so that they *become* together, in reality? This synthesis or bringing together was to be learned in the spirit of the American people, concretized in the Union. Yet, in the face of political sundering along seemingly implacable partisan fissures, what was the reality-based truth that would guide the nation toward its wholeness? Were there policies, new compromises, additional laws or even amendments that would somehow seal the cracks? Or was it rather an existential, historical phenomenon of an entirely different kind? In one sense, we know the answer: it would take a ferocious civil war, a war that perhaps was inevitable. But the war was the result, not the origin of, the phenomenon. Perhaps it was Lincoln himself, the man and character, the leader and learner, who emerged as the existential phenomenon. Several points should be made to illuminate this suggestion.

When the news of Lincoln's election in November of 1860 was telegraphed to the convention in South Carolina, the response was immediate and automatic: On the day of the election they began the process that would lead to secession on December 20. If any of the other three candidates had won or if no one had received a majority of electoral votes—a distinct possibility—this dire move would not have taken place—at least not then. Why? There are scores of reasons, and a hundred variations of historical readings, but the personal character of the victor was surely a fundamental cause. There were no policies, for Lincoln publically denied he had any. There was no threat to the institution of slavery in the South, for the president-elect had promised he would abide by their states' constitutions. Did the South, then, mistrust him? Were the voters in South Carolina more prescient than those in Illinois? Quite to the contrary, the South did trust him, and so did the voters in the North. He was, after all, "Honest Abe." They trusted him as the loyal Unionist whose integrity was the one political constant in an age of compromise. There are great ironies here: the one man who most desired union was the one whose mere presence brought disunion. The pacificists in the North freely—and knowingly—elected the one man who made war inevitable. The North realized Lincoln's election would precipitate secession, and the South knew that, barring some compromise, he would fight. The naïveté, shared by both, was that the conflict would be brief. Only a few were as keen as Sherman, who knew the forthcoming conflict would last for many years. It was the learner of American essence who sparked the conflagration, not by *doing* anything, but simply by his appearance on the scene: he was the avatar of Union, and the Union was the sacred form that enabled the American reality to become the American truth.

Often this spirit of mid-nineteenth century America is depicted in terms of entrepreneurial capitalism, tough-minded frontiersmen, fierce independence, Christianity, and rough-hewn egalitarian politics. But there were other dimensions of a more refined and promising sort. Unknown to Lincoln and most other Americans, a quiet, demure young lady at Amherst was creating poetry of such genius and power it would take a century for it to be accepted and appraised; more publicly recognized, Hawthorne had written one of the finest novels ever, and Melville was pounding out an epic of immense significance. America was no longer the uncouth, tough, and isolated reservoir of Europe's disenfranchised. Its spirit was producing art of the highest quality, especially in the field of literature, all in the unique American idiom. Happily she seemed immune from the more lethal species of speculative ideologies that wold roil Europe forty years later, and already her spirit was emerging as a world persuader. But it was not only in politics and the fine arts that this spirit was changing the world. There was also baseball. This curious, puzzling, alluring entertainment was as American as the Union itself; no other game quite equals its synthesis of teamwork and individual opportunity, wedding both leisure and excitement in a way that endears it to both players and observers. For consider the way the game is played: on the one hand, dazzling executions of double plays or sacrifice bunts seem among the highest achievements of teamwork; but on the other is the rule concerning the line-up: each individual player, all eighteen of them, from the worst to the best, from the runt to the giant, comes to bat at least three times in a full game; and the entire game, at that moment, depends on what he does with that gracefully shaped club. The clumsiest, smallest kid on the sandlot team, or the hitless pitching ace in the majors, each has his supreme moment in which he is the central, dominant figure. The smallest kid, swinging blindly, can bump the ball just over the first baseman's glove; the mighty Casey can strike out. That sweet crack of the bat thrills everyone around the field, and each has the opportunity to make it happen: alone, at bat, the single player is a triumph of individual skill, luck, and wondrous privilege. The game was becoming enormously popular, especially among the young soldiers on both sides in their camps. It seemed so peculiarly American, so integrated to the emerging spirit. From Emily Dickinson to Abner Doubleday, who we were as a people manifested a certain spirit in unity. For Lincoln this spirit was grounded in learnable truth; and it is because of this ground in truth that the man, Lincoln, was spotted by the South, quite correctly, as the phenomenon most likely to thwart their uniqueness, just as he was spotted by the North as the phenomenon that would enable this spirit to flourish, even if it meant war.

Why, though, was the political union deemed necessary for this truth to be learned? There were, after all, Northern moralists who were eager to let the South secede; so evil was slavery they believed the rump Union would be better without it. Lincoln was the learner of the truth who countered this compromise; it was our heritage that revealed the universal truth of inalienable rights, and that the slaves and slaveholders in the South still had those rights; secession would give formal support for the denial of these rights, but the truth of them was still undeniable. Furthermore, the image of two distinct countries splitting the nation in half was a promise of unsuccess and weakness, prey to victimization by larger European powers and further splintering. After the Kansas-Nebraska act the South was rapidly becoming a separate, distinct people; there was already a species of de facto secession if not de jure, and the trends and omens were ominous. Without yet doing anything, simply by being president-elect, the phenomenon of Lincoln as learner was shaping history.

It may seem his learning was slow. He may have noted that the black female had rights because as a person she could think. But was she also a citizen? Even late into the war, Lincoln was considering the problem of what to do with the ex-slaves. He considered sending them voluntarily to a Central American land, or back to Africa. *Them?* It was not until he met their leaders, especially Frederick Douglass, that he learned "they" were a part of "us"; for abused as they were, they saw themselves as American. The war itself had helped: at first Lincoln was reluctant to allow his generals to treat the slaves in occupied territory as contraband—a reluctance based on the uneasy continuation of the border states in the union. Then these black men were allowed to join service units in the army: imagine this—blacks wearing the blue uniform! Then they were allowed to bear arms: blacks wearing blue uniforms with rifles! Then they became noncommissioned officers: black men wearing blue uniforms with stripes on their sleeves; black men giving orders! They always were a part of us—a part of "We the People"; but the truth had to be learned: they were not only free men, they were Americans.

What is so impressive about the first classroom was the manner in which its student studied. The two documents were learnable—"self-evident" in the Enlightenment sense—not merely adoptable as creeds. The provision for amendment in The Constitution and the universality of truth that enabled rights in The Declaration, both invited, even demanded, reflective thinking coupled to social experience. This was government in an original sense: learning what it means to govern and be governed is now part of government itself. But Lincoln had a second classroom to endure.

THE SECOND CLASSROOM

Given the terrible responsibility on Lincoln as commander-in-chief during the Civil War, it is not difficult to elicit sympathy for him. As soon as he was inaugurated the disunion was already underway, and Fort Sumpter was looming as the igniting spark of war. He had no real army in place, the capital city was entirely vulnerable to attack, and the Cabinet was in crisis. He had to act quickly, cautiously, politically, and wisely. Unlike some of his predecessors, such as Washington, Jackson, and Taylor, he had no prior experience as a military general. He was to be molded by the great blacksmith, War, in the furnace of discord, and pummeled by the hammers of grim casualties on the anvils of resolve.

The temptation here is to use the development of the war as an instruction on strategy, tactics, and the special political skills needed for a wartime president. As strategist, his political skills are admired even by most of his enemies both then and now; but it is not such practical wisdom that concerns this inquiry. What does it mean to be commander in chief of the Union during the Civil War? Indeed, what does it mean to be able to make war at all? If the four lessons from the first classroom can be rooted in the seeds planted by the two founding documents, similar lessons can be learned by the husbandry of blood and violence in a seemingly necessary strife between union and disunion. If being brought together for the sake of learnable truths that enable rights itself must be thought, so too must the will to keep that union intact by armed violence be *thought*. The learning in the second classroom of the war years should not be seen as the advantage of practical experience. The events of the war can be read as part of our shared history; but the truth that is found only in confronting what it means for these events to be endured as a cruel but necessary husbandry does not follow from the shift to active engagement or even to noting chronology. The spiritual reality of the Union was, prior to 1860, incomplete. This incompleteness was not caused merely by the existence of slavery, though the discord caused by the political struggle over its status was surely a catalyst. Rather, its incompleteness lies in the need for a very special species of sacrifice, without which what it means to be unified as we are is literally unlearnable. For such a union cannot merely be bestowed by appeal to principle; indeed not even the noble sacrifices of those who gave their lives on behalf of independence were able to establish the truth. There are hundreds of wars in the history books that can reveal to us what it means for one people to fight with trained armies against another people; there are also many remarkable civil wars, such as England's in the 1640s, that show us what it means to be one nation severed by differences that only armed conflicts can resolve; but there is only one war like this one—and why this is so is a truth we must learn, as Lincoln also had to learn. What makes the American Civil War unique as a resource for learning requires that it be seen as revealing universal truth concretized in existential individuality. In order to let the truth emerge, a brief sketch divided on six existentially significant phases may guide: (1) from Fort Sumpter on April 12, 1861, to the first Bull Run or Manassas on July, 21; (2) from Bull Run to Shiloh on April 1862; (3) from Shiloh to Antietam on September 17, 1862; (4) from these to Gettysburg and Vicksburg of July 4, 1863; (5) from these victories to the horrors of Cold Harbor on June 3 of the following year; until (6) finally Appomattox on April 9, 1865. The Gettysburg-Vicksburg victories mark the apex, center, and turning point of the conflict, in which the rebellion was marked for defeat, yet the long, ugly two-year finishing, the naked attrition of the beleaguered, seemed perversely necessary. Even those of us who merely read about it can feel its burden: we shall never be the same.

1. It is remarkable how many people, both North and South, including Lincoln, believed that Beauregard's guns at Fort Sumpter began what would be at most a six-month conflict. The rout at Bull Run–Manassas shattered that naïveté, but its rude awakening did not keep the president from seeing beyond the shame: true, his green troops needed better training and discipline, but they were not cowards, nor were all his commanders bereft of leadership. It was now clear the war would be protracted, and because it promised to be an extended conflict, a long-term strategy, enabled by an improved command structure, was imperative. It was precisely these two factors, command and strategy, that fell heavily on Lincoln as a lesson to be learned. The command was his: he was commander in chief. How was he to think about this so as to act wisely about it? We are now accustomed to the role of a presidential commander in chief; his duty seems to be threefold: appointing the best men to conduct the war, supporting them with all the power of the government, and providing the overall strategy on both political and military levels. One thinks of Roosevelt's happy reliance on George Marshall throughout the entire Second World War, or Wilson's continuing trust on Pershing in the First. For Lincoln, however, both the strategy and command were elusive, for the very reason the conflict had occurred in the first place: confusion about the reality. Perhaps it was because Lincoln had read Clausewitz, but in any event his own grasp of the theoretical, overall strategy was remarkably sound; indeed at times a reader of this history may feel the president alone grasped the essentials: he could not, surprisingly, make his military leaders understand the simple logic of it, just as he could not convince the prewar politicians of the American essence. It was Lincoln who realized from the very beginning what others seemed to miss or grasp only vaguely: this war had to be aggressive, tough, and destructive. He saw that it was the Confederate armies and not Richmond or any other city that mattered, that commanders should fight rather than maneuver to avoid

conflicts; that the blockade (and hence the Mississippi) was essential; that the Federal army could lose a battle—indeed many battles—without losing the war; but they could lose the war by not engaging in battles they would not win; that offence was necessary since the Confederacy needed only to be left alone; that the need to attack entailed a higher risk of casualties, and that the new technologies were forcing a new level of brutality that simply had to be endured. He knew these things; but both his political and military leaders around him could not grasp them, or were unwilling to embrace them. Yet, as commander in chief it was his responsibility to enforce the strategy: he alone had the legitimate authority. He was a skilled politician, so why, knowing the validity of his basic strategy, was he unable to enforce it earlier? He had to learn what he already knew. Part of this learning was of himself: he had to learn to be commander in chief before what he knew as the proper strategy could become real. The temptation to be resisted is to view this merely as a problem in shifting from theory to practice; we should not diminish the importance of this learning by suggesting Lincoln knew the strategic theory but had difficulty putting it into practice. It was not merely that the president had to overcome resistance to his plans, but that in the torment of doing so he learned the meaning of what he already knew. For he became not merely abler, but wiser in a philosophical sense.

2. Though routed, the federal armies gained much from Bull Run and the Confederate armies lost much by their assumption of invincibility. Shiloh was a shock for both sides: it was a narrow but first decisive victory in a major battle for the North; it revealed the peculiar qualities of Grant and Sherman; it pointed out that the West was at least equal to, or perhaps even greater in importance than, the privileged real estate of Virginia; and—it was horrific in its bloodshed. Lincoln discovered from Shiloh the cruelest need of all: the endurance of, and the need to inflict, enormous casualties. This wisdom first emerges as a political-military realization: given what Lincoln called the "arithmetic," the North should win. As a purely strategic principle, one could see the two salient facts: offence always requires a larger force and usually larger casualties than defense, except in quick attacks, later to be known as *Blitzkriegen.* The North had greater numbers of soldiers, and a greater industrial base, so their need to attack could be sustained; thus the "arithmetic" should result in a federal victory, even if the South were blessed by more brilliant tactical generals. But it was more than mere strategy to ask: what does it mean to endure and inflict huge casualties? What magic, trickery, or perhaps denuding honesty could convince mothers from Maine or Wisconsin to send their sweet, vulnerable children into the grim and devouring maw of this feral attrition, and turn them into killers? Indeed, how could Lincoln himself endure it? They did, and he did; Shiloh established that truth: it was a truth that enabled us to learn what it means to be ourselves.

3. It was not endurance, however, that plagued the commander in chief from Shiloh to Antietam; it was the lack of offensive spirit necessary to put the "arithmetic" to work, and this was embodied in that avatar of hesitation, Gen. George McClellan. After the first Battle of Bull Run, everyone knew the army needed discipline and training, and this McClellan clearly provided. But once achieved, his splendid army was not allowed victory. For the reader of history, McClellan's almost criminal reluctance to engage the enemy is agonizing; for Lincoln it was existential anguish. On a visit to the army, Lincoln saw the mighty host and remarked in astonishment that this was McClellan's body-guard. Is not Lincoln, as commander in chief, partly responsible for this non-performance? Since he alone had the power to appoint, he recognized he was partly responsible; but more deeply he realized he was learning to be commander in chief. His delay in this erudition was as cruel as McClellan's delays. His attempts to micromanage the war proved feckless. It was Antietam, ironically, that allowed him to do two things: fire McClellan, and sign the Emancipation Proclamation. At first both acts seemed hollow, for McClellan's replacements, Pope, Burnside, and Hooker, were as bad, if not worse until Meade took over; and the proclamation seemed hollow, since de facto it freed no slave. The proclamation was signed on the thin disguise that Antietam was a victory, McClellan was fired on the thin disguise that Antietam was a failure. Nevertheless, the signing and the firing marked a turn in the cruel education: Lincoln was learning what he already knew by the irresistability of paradox, and paradoxes were prolific. The dreadful casualties at the creek were revealing in their pain, but the willingness of the soldiers and the nation to continue the bloodletting was a newer kind of pain. The question was not how long they could endure, the question was to understand what it means to endure at all. Was it the "cause"? The signing of the proclamation is often suggested by historians that the cause itself was changing, from unionism to emancipation; though Lincoln himself realized the first implied the second. The cause, however, in itself, did not seem adequate; certainly the cause, however noble, could not provide the tutelage to teach him the truth of his own learning.

4. The twin victories at Vicksburg and Gettysburg changed not only the military picture, but also the political one. Lee had made a dreadful error, and Meade had artfully taken advantage of it; but it was Grant's victory that mattered, for it revealed the true nature of the upcoming struggle and ultimate triumph: only by hard, tough, and bitter persistence and resoluteness could the entrenched defender be ferreted out. The new warfare was not to be won by tactical brilliance, but by relentless, strategic attrition. Time, casualties, and setbacks simply could not be allowed to matter. The Confederacy was now forever split, the Mississippi flowed "unvexed," the behemoth armies of Sherman and Grant came from West to East, and their prodigious weight could only be delayed, not stopped. Somewhere in this transition

Lincoln learned as commander in chief, not by the victories, but by what enabled them. He learned the true meaning of the endurance, the acceptance of casualties, and the perpetration of a harsher warfare. It was not the legitimacy of the cause that justified the sacrifice, but the sacrifice itself that enobled the war. The etymological origin of the word is *sacra-facere*: to make holy; the courage, the pain, the blood, the ruin of glorious youth, and the fretting of command and obedience were bringing about an absolute imperative to continue; for the fallen, though now mute, cried out that their personal loss need not be in vain. Was it possible for the President to say this openly: *their* sacrifice demanded *our* sacrifice: it is not we but they who hallow the ground? This is not mere oratory; it is learning transformational truth.

In the victories, Lincoln saw once again, but on a deeper level, that to be a warrior it is not enough to sacrifice one's life; much harder is to learn to kill. To take upon oneself the terrible burden of slaying another human being in wartime is not a mere moral question of justification; it requires a profound sense that who we are matters, and consequently who "they" are, as those threatening the institution that enables as to be who we are, must be defeated. The warrior must develop a fierce instinct for the jugular, a sense of the enemy's vulnerability, and the raw power to strike and damage. To instill these killer instincts in ground troops is what drill sergeants are all about, and these unsung trainers are as important as any in the army; but to *adopt* such feral urgencies as part of one's character as supreme warrior may be the harshest lesson of all. It seems so perverse: to become a killer because of love, not only the love of what is ours, but the love of victory, the love of triumph for its own sake, the love of peace, but above all, a love of ourselves, as individuals and as mankind. It is only because of this achievement of being a warrior that the president was able to share the truth of what it meant in the Gettysburg Address.

5. Cold Harbor stunned even Ulysses S. Grant. It was not merely the mushrooming casualties, but what was happening to the boys: they pinned pieces of paper on their uniforms with their names, so sure were they that they would not see the next dawn. Two things appall us by the image: the grim fatalism of the doomed soldiers who yet did their gruesome task, and the stark resolve of the new commander. There are some historians who look upon Grant as a simple butcher, feeding his soldiers as cannon fodder into the costly fray, impervious to the need for tactical maneuver. Here was a man whose first name was that of one of the great heros in Homer's epic of the Trojan War, who had with sheer, dogged persistence, hung on at Donelson, Shiloh, Vicksburg, and Chattanooga; a victor in each of these important battles, but one whose methods seemed at worst, barbaric, at best, plodding. It was this seeming heartless, relentless, unrefined, and callous westerner to whom Lincoln had given supreme command, in an act unparalled in our history. The government, including the secretary of war and the commander

in chief himself, ceded to Grant all authority: they would not even *ask* what Grant would do; they simply provided the warlord with what he needed to succeed. After Gettysburg we see a new Lincoln: he was no longer the mere unionist or emancipator or even the force behind his commanders; he had become the conqueror. He had to defeat the enemy however long it took; and the three generals who were willing to fight in this new way, Sheridan, Sherman, and Grant, had been unleashed as the dogs of the war. It was not pretty. Grant himself admitted Cold Harbor was a terrible mistake. Yet, in a way, it was inevitable. Lee, the victor, shuddered at it; not only because of the slaughter, but because of its portent: nothing would stop this man. There is something almost inhuman about the new federal commander's ability to absorb all those losses on so many battlefields, yet to continue the inevitable drift toward Richmond and the critical rail lines that were so vital to the shredded Confederacy. What is often overlooked is that Grant was Lincoln's military alter ego. The president had at last found the one man who grasped the essence of the war: the sacrifices were misspent if the rebellion was not entirely buried. The nation of, for, and by the people, "would not perish from the earth." That possibility—which at times appeared almost inevitable—had transformed Lincoln: to keep the nation from perishing was the supreme issue; it had become a sacred need. Cold Harbor had been gruesome. The men had become fatalist zombies but the Gettysburg Address had revealed the truth: we as a nation must survive.

6. The scene shifts from Grant at the siege of Richmond to Sherman in Georgia, and to a lesser extent, on Sheridan in the valley. What was this new warfare becoming? There was devastation of American land, destruction of civilian property, and ruination of vast expanses having no overt military value. This was war as punitive, designed to kill the spirit of secession, not merely to conquer its armies. Yet, in a curious way, it was a war that revealed war's essence. Any attempt to make war a polite or decent endeavor must be purged: it was after all, the noble and gentlemanly Lee who slaughtered the youthful troops at Cold Harbor. If the savagery of Sherman in Georgia and Grant in Virginia stuns us with the horrors of the new warfare, the generosity and grace of these icy killers at the peace tables stun as well. Rarely has a peace been more forgiving, more healing, more noble than at Appomattox. The new primitive war of devastation and attrition was sire to the new peace: rewelcoming the prodigal. Their property was returned, their status as states eventually reestablished, their horses and rifles went with them as they trudged back to their farms. On the surface it seems as if the war and the peace were entirely in service of the cause, the cause of the Union, the cause so nobly presented in the Gettysburg Address. Perhaps. But the term "cause" may not be adequate; for there could be other causes. Truth, or essence, may serve us

better: the truth of what it means to be American was what was learned, and by none so deeply as the president himself.

What Lincoln learned from the two classrooms he already knew: that is, in the first classroom the two documents were already written and familiar to most Americans; in the second classroom, the Clausewitzean principles of war and Lincoln's grasp of the "arithmetic" were available prior to Bull Run; when the strategy became the guiding success of a new war, however, they revealed themselves as truths enabling the Gettysburg Address. In this way, we learn what we had learned. Is this mere reiteration? Does it harken back to Plato's suggestion in the *Meno* that knowledge is recollection? Or is it akin to a young musician learning first the use of the bow, and then the pressure points on his instrument, before learning to play the violin? Or is the key paradox? I must first know in order to learn, not learn in order to know. Perhaps all of these suggestions contribute. Whatever we suggest, however, it is clear that the second learning is not the same as the first. If we Americans already knew what we learned in the war, then what is altered is not what we know but who the knower becomes. However we conceive of it, it seems clear by this reflection on Lincoln as *learner* that what is "new" in any "second learning" is being real as true. For the sake of this inquiry the present chapter cannot be taken out of the context of inquiry: we ask, is it possible to learn what is already learned? Lincoln can be seen as one who learns his own learning from what he already knew, though the truth of the second learning is a transformation of the learner.

The brief reflection on the war's lessons enables us to suggest the following: if Washington, Jefferson, Hamilton, et al., were the *founding* fathers, Lincoln and his colleagues were the *transforming* sons, and this transforming is a metaphysical one, enabling, as the president said over the graves of the fallen, a *new birth* of freedom; we as a nation, as a people, are transformed.

SEVEN

The Student

The unwarned innocently signs up for an undergraduate course in metaphysics. Perhaps he was attracted by the term itself, for it sounds a bit mysterious and profound; in all likelihood he has met the word before, and knows vaguely about its topics. From the texts it appears to be a study of alternative theories, not unlike the theories of government he had learned in political science or the alternative theories of light or the origin of our universe considered in his science classes. This impression is reinforced by the early lectures, in which the theories are identified and explained: Aristotle, Descartes, Kant, Russell—the task seemed to be to learn how these people explain the world and ourselves. There were arguments of a sort that refuted or supported, just as there were in science or art history or economics. Yet, if he is intelligent and sensitive enough he realizes there may be a difference. *I think, therefore I am. The unexamined life is not worth living. To be is to be perceived. Being is not an entity. Space and time are forms of sensibility. This piece of chalk is white may be true, but this piece of chalk takes up space, must be true. Contingency and necessity are of necessity distinct.* These are not merely "sayings," opinions, or theories: they have a peculiar relevance and significance about us as thinkers. The emphasis upon reason makes it seem as if philosophy is akin to science and mathematics; but the singular impression that their reasoning becomes our reasoning, that we ourselves become involved in the tension of competing ways of thinking and feeling, makes the class more like poetry or drama, in which intense, personal identification is made with the hopeless Othello or the fated Juliet, torturing love itself. We do not say that because Descartes thinks, he therefore exists; we say: I think, so I must exist.

As youngsters in school we are taught the world is made up of tiny entities called atoms. As we grow and learn, we ask: but what makes up the atoms themselves? We listen to those who say such dividing is unlimited:

there is no reason, we are told, why any one level of smallness itself cannot be further divided. That makes sense. Or does it? The unsuspecting under-graduate is asked to study the passage on Kant's antinomies, where he reads that both the assertion there must be an ultimate particle, and the assertion that division of particles into ever smaller ones is indefinite, are both *false*. How can they both be false? A picture in the newspaper shows a newly discovered subatomic entity, smaller than the one discovered a few years before. Surely if it can be reproduced by an electron microscope, and I see its magnification, must it not also be made up of smaller things? Yes, of course; but we are able to say that just because the particle is now in some sense experienced, to suggest there must be further divisions beyond what is expe-rienced is not based on anything testable, but on pure speculation. This warning against a misuse of a faculty or one way of thinking is not really about particulate matter anymore; it is about our own powers of cognition, and hence our own reality. Perhaps nature and the study of nature is not all there is, for it is not nature that reveals our faculties.

The student reads other texts. Happiness itself seems now a problem. Perhaps being free makes us less happy; would we reject the former for the latter? There is another fear that follows from this: a life of bovine satisfac-tion, or even drug-induced tranquility, seems somehow unworthy. Perhaps, though, freedom is too high a price to pay. Whether it is or is not, however, may not move us as much as the realization that it is we who consider such things, not merely as a weighing of opinions, but as a resource for learning truth. And what is the worth of *that*? Why does truth matter? If I could choose a life of considerable pleasure and satisfaction based on a lie, or a life of wretched confusion and anguish in the search for elusive truth, would I not choose . . . well? Which would we choose?

These are deep and troubling matters, to be sure; and perhaps the young student is uplifted or at least excited by them. But are they not to be found elsewhere as well? Do not great poets, dramatists, theologians, even social theorists, provide the same? To read the novelist Dostoyevski may afford access to similar profundity; Milton's epic may teach us about freedom and evil more intimately than Leibniz, Shakespeare's *Sonnets* may show us more about love than Plato's *Symposium*. Modern astronomy surely does more to dispel bad cosmology than Kant's critique of it. And so we may admit that the course in metaphysics, though worthy, is not exclusive. There is nothing to suggest that a course in metaphysics offers anything not available by other means. Since the number of people who enroll in metaphysics courses is, given the vastness of the global population, almost infinitesimally small, is it not arrogance of the grossest sort to claim that it alone offers the species of wisdom that is ultimate and transformational?

Yet, it is not clear that the poets, novelists, and dramatists offer what a study of metaphysics provides. The student realizes a specific fact. This fact is that there are certain books in our libraries that are seriously read by intelligent and erudite people; these books are on metaphysics. This fact needs explanation. Why do many profound nonphilosophers as well as philosophers or students read these books? Perhaps they are all deluded; but this suggestion itself requires a suspension of normal judgment and is entertained merely as an assurance we are aware of abstract possibilities that are highly unlikely. Indeed, this kind of provisional scepticism is made most frequently by philosophers themselves. The point remains that very wise people in many fields do indeed read works on metaphysics. These works are read by many of the great contributors in the fields that seem to overlap or at least echo what the philosophers consider. Melville was profoundly influenced by Kant, Thomas Mann and Richard Wagner by Schopenhauer, Voltaire wrote *Candide* to refute Leibniz; the theologian Thomas Aquinas was influenced greatly by Aristotle. Yet, the study of metaphysics as a discipline in philosophy is not a consideration of influences. There is something that happens in the classroom or seminar that is not entirely reducible to anything else: it is sui generis. If the professor is of any worth, the positions or theories are not merely presented, they are offered as ways of reasoning about reality. We can learn to do this by first following wise predecessors; but insofar as we reflect on the truth as such, our own reasoning and our own ability to criticize and affirm becomes independent of the text. That there should be a special discipline, requiring special training, in which such critical reasoning is yoked to our ability to ask profound questions about the meaning of reality itself, may be justified on the ground that such thinking is both difficult and meaningful. Because it is difficult we need the long tradition of the history of philosophy and an expert to help us read them; because it is meaningful we need to develop our own ability to think and to wonder. It does not seem, then, entirely unjustified to develop a discipline having its own status. If it does have its own status, however, perhaps although Dostoyevski and Milton are invaluable in showing us how to think and feel about freedom and evil, they do not provide the same level that a philosophical inquiry into their metaphysical meanings can do. In what way does an organized class on metaphysics offer what is unique?

The professor, early in the semester, points out that the inquiry they study is ultimate: there is no higher discipline that must be presupposed. Words such as *fundamental, basic, first order,* and *foundational* are also used to suggest the originary autonomy of metaphysics; similes, such as Descartes' likening metaphysics to the root of a tree whose branches are the other the disciplines may also help. The very claim of ultimacy becomes itself a critical device: if a purported metaphysical account is shown merely to follow what is learned by another discipline, membership in the elitist club is forfeit. What is fundamental, however, is not merely a few judgments that a thinker may propose; rather, the very methodology and critical procedure of the entire approach must be designed and conceived so as to warrant justification for ultimacy. The student may note that most metaphysicians belabor their method almost as much as their doctrines. However well or badly it is done, metaphysics in principle originates, rather than follows, all other questioning, though this origination is not temporal, but formal.

Argumentation about the fundamental is required for it to be fundamental. Yet arguments against established positions seem easier and more persuasive than those that support, leading the unwary to a certain sceptical attitude. Any generalized proposition needs only one counterinstance to be disproven: is not the claim that all men can think invalidated by one man who is comatose or severely handicapped by neurological trauma? One albino crow undermines the claim all crows are black. A systematic account of all that is real is therefore extremely vulnerable, for under critique it seems such accounts must beg the question about the range of the term "all." Yet, this seeming advantage for the skeptical critic is misleading. The ultimacy of metaphysics does not rely on the success of any one particular account; indeed that there are criticisms may often be seen as a refinement rather than a rejection—and even if a rejection is warranted, that too is an advance. We do not want false positions to mislead us.

It is not only ultimacy but authority that seems to provide metaphysical inquiry with its allure. Often this authority seems entirely dependent on rational critique. The student may regard an established religion or a popular ideology with a certain degree of respect or even persuasion, for both religions and ideologies may have internal consistency and may bring to our state of confusion certain needed guidelines for behavior and assessment. Yet the critical, dialectical procedures of philosophy afford access to the asking of fundamental questions not offered by either religion or ideology. It does not matter that the student may continue to believe in his creed or ideology, it is merely enough for him to recognize that the search for truth is distinct from a belief in a truth. What at first may seem an irritant or even a disappointment—that philosophy does not seem to resolve great questioning but intensifies it—may, upon reflection, offer a kind of allure different from any doctrine whatsoever.

Critique and argumentation surely give some authority to the metaphysical discipline; yet logical proofs of themselves cannot account either for our understanding of reality or even for the authority in metaphysical thinking. Certainly, deductive proof cannot be ultimate since such proofs require premises, and their origin is beyond the mere rules of inference. Even if we add induction, or the broader experience of a richly endowed, self-examined life, the mere adherence to any procedure that requires laws, principles, or canons of analysis cannot be both ultimate and authorative at the same time. The undergraduate student may sense this fairly early; his own reality is not only the object of his inquiry, it is also the source of it. Ultimately, then, the basis of metaphysical authority is not the application of codified procedures, but their origin in our own being real as thoughtful. It is not the code or even the codification, but that we are the codifiers that authorizes metaphysics. Yet a moment's reflection shows that we are not merely codifiers of our own thinking; we are also the fundamental problem or topic of our reasoning, and this realization forces us to recognize that we, in our myriad ways, present ourselves to ourselves as problems, or perhaps better, as questions. The discovery of the propriety of our reasoning is therefore only a part of our authority, for as authority we blame and praise, censure and affirm, rejoice and regret. Perhaps, indeed, the codification of methods and inferences is at best a propadeutic; even the awareness that we ourselves can codify is not as fundamental as the realization that we need to do so. Our problems become our authority—for it is in part because we have problems that we need to think at all—yet we cannot say from this that therefore metaphysics is problem solving. Indeed if by the term "problem" we mean what can, in principle, be *resolved*, then the term may be a distraction; hence the second term of the disjunct, "questioning," may be preferable. We become question-worthy in part because we question. This too adds to the authority in metaphysics.

What then, is the *lure*? If problem solving in the sense of discovering solutions to practical or theoretical snarls is not the primary goal, then why engage in such a toilsome and prodigious effort? Is not truth, by definition, always a closure? Why search for what cannot be found? This question deceives: we do find a great deal; indeed we actually come to know certain things by philosophical inquiry—but such discovery is always an opening to wider or deeper reflection; new paradoxes emerge, not because our inquiry makes us dumber, but because it make us smarter. The lure itself, therefore, subtly but profoundly changes: we seek to become wise—which is a truth-directed virtue—and not merely to know. We seek to be transformed. But how?

A midterm paper is assigned. The student is surprised to find so many criticisms, and discusses it with the professor. His are not factual errors; nor are they violations of logic. Rather, he is shown that the interconnection of arguments must coalesce on the nature of the question. What does it mean that Descartes distinguishes body from mind on the basis of the differences in our knowledge: since perceiving is not the same as conceiving, body must be different from mind. His analysis must be challenged, of course, but the tactic itself deserves our reflection: do we truly realize perception is not conception? If so, why must this epistemic difference ground a metaphysical one? Even if Descartes is wrong, the reasons for his error must have a status; and if Descartes can be justified, those reasons too are of a special quality. How do we think like this? What is happening to us when we learn in a class on metaphysics to evaluate such fundamental truth critically?

As thinkers, all people are able to reflect on their own being real. Not all, however, do so; of those that do, not all do so with authority and ultimacy.

Once having done so, the ability to do it is not an abstract possibility but a possibility grounded in actuality. The ontological shift from the ground of possibility in abstraction to possibility in our own reality brings about a metaphysical transformation, in which the truth of what it means to be real replaces a construct of how to externalize being real. Does this transformation occur *only* in philosophy classes in a classroom? No, to be sure; but the structure of a class may be an overlooked though worthy model, for in class-rooms the authority (in the professor) and the learning (in the student) from the texts (putting us *already* in the metaphysical world) provide an actual, observable phenomenon open to analysis as true, hence ultimate. The student, armed with the critique of his midterm, is now assigned the final term paper. As he struggles with the metaphysical topic, his own reflection on his own being real plays a newer role; he is more central than the literature even though his grasp of the texts may have been the resource for his becoming central. He is "doing" metaphysics. We speak of "doing" history rather than "making" history, distinguishing the Roman emperors as making history and Tacitus from doing history. Yet, even this distinction is troubling, for Gibbon may also to some extent *make* history by the way he *does* history, since his work on the fall of the Roman empire had such a powerful affect on the eighteenth and nineteenth centuries. "Doing" philosophy however, unlike history, always also "makes" philosophy. The undergraduate discovers this: his thinking about reality is truly making reality different: it is transforming, just as facing fear transforms fear into courage.

Is writing a term paper doing metaphysics? It can be. The very structure of a paper requires the student to set up the problem, show the seeming paradoxes inherent in it, note the contributions of the authors he has read, evaluate them critically, and then write a summary conclusion. Perhaps he even includes his own analysis. This seeming pedantic process is a boon, for it provides a way not only of presentation but of discovery. In doing it he is making it. Adherence even to such academic forms provides him with a way of turning vague and amorphous insights into a defensible, and hence illuminating, discovery. More important, however, his actual performance changes who he is, for he has confronted his own being real with some degree of authority, and since it is his personal reality that is questioned, it is ultimate. There is no guarantee that the student will continue to learn in this way, nor is the suggestion made that his achievement ranks with the great and lasting works; it is enough to recognize that his own being real is forever altered by his examination of what it means to be real, for having done it he knows it is concretely, not abstractly, possible. This change is not unlike the loss of innocence—a theme that will be discussed further in the next chapter—and hence deserves to be called a transformation. All this merely because a student writes a term paper on metaphysics? The academic setting provides a model that makes it possible, not necessary. Nevertheless we must ask: assuming the student has indeed glimpsed his own being real in an ultimate and authoritative way, what is the nature of his transformation?

Some religious conversions are characterized as personal transformations or epiphanies, so that the convert speaks of himself as a new man. There is no need to be sceptical or contemptuous about this: we can see that the life he lives after the conversion is radically distinct, perhaps even improved, from the life he lived before. He experiences a deep joy, he feels saved or redeemed, his behavior is now more generous, more decent, more exciting. So far-reaching are these changes that he feels compelled to attribute them to an external influence, usually divine; he thus deems them as a gift or bestowal. Yet it is he who makes the leap of faith, he who embraces the new religious spirit. It would be churlish to deny his being transformed, but whether or not this transformation is metaphysical is less obvious. His is certainly a psychological change; his emotions seem to play a greater role than his thought, and unlike the philosophical learner, there is no claim to universality in the change itself, though the believer certainly may maintain the tenants he holds are universally true. But the convert's transformation, powerful and meaningful as it may be, is itself not necessarily wrought by doing metaphysics. Metaphysical transformation, we learn, can be achieved only by metaphysics itself. The seeming boldness and even arrogance of this claim may be muted slightly by the realization that metaphysical thinking is not restricted to university classrooms; but even with this admission the outrage seethes like the angry grumbling of an affronted audience ready, but not yet committed, to booing and throwing tomatoes. Whether the performance should be pelted with condign censure rests upon whether the boldness of the stagecraft is coupled to the validity of the work. Were one to poll the populace of professors teaching such courses it is highly likely most would deny that metaphysical truth is achieved only by metaphysics. Yet if this same poll were to ask further if the study of metaphysics includes an inquiry into what metaphysics is, the majority might agree. What would it mean to suggest a metaphysical transformation could occur *without* doing metaphysics? Were this possible we would have to assume externality as the anchor for our being real. The externality of our being real would then be understood as an event caused in space and time, no different in kind from natural phenomena. But natural phenomena are rendered thinkable by constructs; they are not directly recognized as our own being real. But the converse is also true: to make metaphysics is to do metaphysics. Thinking about my own reality means my reality is capable of being thought about, and this spotlighting or denuding necessarily alters being real: it is a transformation of the metaphysical reality (me) wrought by the discovery of what it means to be inquirer and inquired about.

The metaphysical transformation wrought and discovered by the student in the classroom may be accompanied by certain passions, just as is the change wrought in the religious convert. Some students do indeed get excited by their discovery, and may even express this emotion, claiming their lives had been changed (for the good, usually). The nature of this passion has already been scanned in the chapter on wonder. But it is not the emotions that reveal the nature of the learning. Usually the passionate element is less sudden than that of the convert's; it develops over a longer period and is often more subtle, though no less powerful. There are some emotional benefits: the learner may find himself more secure, a sense of pride or self-worth may follow from the realization of his power to do what he is doing. He may take pleasure in the sheer loftiness and nobility of the enterprise. There are negative passions, however, as well: anxiety may increase, a sense of loneliness may result from the recognition of the rarity of his concerns, and sceptical doubt may trouble him. These changes, however, are psychological; and though they cannot or at least should not be dismissed, their consideration threatens to reduce the metaphysical act to phenomena; indeed emotivism always lurks in the wings of this philosophical drama. Does it boil down to this: some of us like doing what is called philosophy, and this liking is its ultimate justification? That relatively few thinkers make such condescending analyses does not bar the indictment from the prosecutorial briefs; we need only remember that indictments await trials and judgment. Why, though, given their danger, should the passions be mentioned at all? Even if there were no harm in mentioning them, are they not distractions from the purity of the rational, metaphysical critique?

In almost every philosophical age, the formalists among us tend to deprecate emotion or what are called "feelings." Since we can be deceived about our feelings, it seems we should not rely on them. We may genuinely believe, for example, that we love our father, but a therapist can show us what we think is love is "really" fear. The young often confuse desire with love, the criminal may so feign honesty as to actually believe his lies, the racist may refuse to accept the accomplishments of the hated, the sensitive may confuse guilt with shame; self-esteem may actually mask self-loathing. Given the massive self-deception about feelings, they are rightly judged as unreliable for any actual, given state. Yet this epistemic imprecision is not entirely wanton. If I am afraid, one cannot convince me that really I am not afraid but hungry; even if we may be misled in our own evaluation, such errors do not equate jealousy with friendship or joy with greed or pleasure with disgust. A therapist may show us our self-deception, but such showing itself reveals that the first evaluation was false and the second, true. In this sense, feelings are no different from external perceptions: I may see water in the desert, but it is a mirage. There are critical techniques that help us to rely on our senses, and there are ways to help us understand our true feelings. Terror is different from amusement, though we may be amused at a scary film. The passionate element in our own being real is needful: suppose, for example, I recognize that being able to be guilty is an essential modality of our being real; I further distinguish 'feeling guilty' from 'being guilty.' Yet, guilt as felt is part of what it means to be guilty; the distinction is required because those who are guilty but do not feel guilty may be sociopathic, and those who feel guilty but who are not, may be mentally disturbed or overly scrupulous; such cases do nor forfeit the philosophical significance of our feeling guilty when in fact we are guilty. If, for example, we discover that feeling burdened is a characteristic of feeling guilty, we may well want to suggest that what it means to be able to be burdened is of fundamental importance for understanding what it means to be real. The philosopher must be cautious about relying on particular feelings as an epistemic resource for specific modes of existence, but what it means to feel such emotions is surely a legitimate resource for inquiring into our reality. If I do not know what it means to feel guilty I cannot understand what it means to be guilty; though if I were deprived of knowing the feeling I still might be able to realize that I am guilty. Thus, an amoral and insensitive sociopath may realize that, as the author of a harmful crime he will, if caught, be punished, even if he feels no guilt at all. He knows he is the cause of the harm but not that he is the *agent* of it. Yet such a morally depraved and deprived person could not succeed in doing metaphysics, since felt guilt is necessary for comprehending what it means to be guilty, and being guilty is essential to being a person. To include feelings in metaphysical thinking does not automatically engage the academic or clinical disciplines of psychology, for we neither speculate about the causes nor seek to cure a disease. Poets and dramatists speak of passions, but neither in a causal nor curative way. The philosopher includes feelings not to dress up his learning with practical application, but because our own being real is already richly revealed as caring and vulnerable; a purely formal construct such as an abstractly conceived mind or a physical substance with only variable properties of sentiment attached to it cannot account for our own being real: we are real as passionate, and this realization in no way lessens the authority or fundamentality of metaphysical learning. The only caveat that need be made is not to equate metaphysical transformation with a mere shift in sentiment or a response to a powerful emotional reaction. A student may be excited by philosophical learning, but the excitement in itself is not the basis for understanding the transformation; at the same time it is entirely legitimate to suggest that discovering what it means to be real may excite us, and the nature and meaning of that excitement may well be a part of our being real.

One advantage of considering an actual university course in metaphysics is the prolonged and sustained effort for the length of a semester. Whatever passionate need may be required for metaphysics, it is unlike the sudden, sweeping, and passing flights occasioned by artworks or one-time discussions, or even from intense feelings about human events, such as surprise or sudden panic. The semester offers a developed, reflective approach to profound inquiry; the depth of the question demands a lengthy and reiterative discovery, reinforced by repetition and rethinking. There may be moments of enlightenment; but usually even these are the product of sustained reconfrontations, as students often remark: "Ah, *now* I see where this is leading," knowing full well the burst of daylight results from long periods of working in predawn shadows. The excitement then, that comes from such discovery, is a triumph achieved by extended preparation, akin to the piano student able to weave the fugue together as a single piece only after struggling to master the individual voices first. As such, it is a triumph *earned* as well as bestowed—the protracted effort does not merely add to its worth, it becomes essential for its truth. Thus, the moment at which the student says "Aha! I see it now," is decisively not the moment of transformation; rather the entire semester, including even the periods of boredom when the professor drones on about an irrelevant point, is transforming—indeed the transformation may yet be incomplete at semester's end. What the participation in a semester-long inquiry into being real can do, however, is to open up a hitherto unexpected potentiality in which to *think* about being becomes a thinking *as* being. This thinking is, as was noted earlier, sui generis just because it neither appeals to prior, independently established principles learned elsewhere, nor does it rely upon constructs or theoretical systems to account for who we are. Since our own being real is what we learn to think about, no theoretical construct can precede it. Yet, neither is such learning reduced to mere empirical observation or personal intuitions about the inner self or soul. In all thinking there is, to be sure, a reach for unity, as Kant points out in the Transcendental Deduction; and this unity, insofar as it is at least partially derived from reasoning, must have formal elements; but since this inquiry is by definition, original, what it means to unify formally is itself open to learning.

Metaphysics is learning what it means to be real. In the academic sense it may be characterized as the formal study of reality. The truth of being real (reality) is akin though not identical to the meaning of being real, in the sense that truth or meaning is what enables us to think about our reality with authority. The only direct access we have to reality is our own being real, but this learning is concretely universal. For the existence of external entities I am restricted to theoretical constructs of their occurrence, and hence can never grasp their essence or reality. Further, my own being real is not solipsistic, for who I am includes my being in the world and my belonging with others; the egocentric, denuded entity of a single mind is a misleading abstraction that stems from ranking entities above being real. Yet my uniqueness is essential for learning metaphysical truth: I cannot escape my own personal guilt shared by no one else any more than I can escape my own pleasure. The realization that being real can be thought about is transformational, that is: it requires a reciprocity of the learner and the learned. Metaphysical truth cannot be obtained by mere receptivity, as if there were a pure subject that is informed by various epistemic operations about external events or objects. Furthermore, an entirely receptivist accounting of our learning necessarily ranks our ability to recognize that something is or happens as the cardinal achievement, so that anything we may add to the mere fact that something exists is entirely arbitrary and without authority, for such assessments would lie beyond the mechanisms of receiving purely empirical data. Not only would metaphysics itself be made impossible—for I could only learn what I receive and never be able to go beyond my reception of it to the reality of it—but all nonfactual claims, assertions, judgments, or evaluations would stem from a single, isolated consciousness without authority to discover in them any universally significant truth.

If our own being real, now expanded to a richness by the awareness of being in the world, is to be *thought*, the question is, What form must the asking take? Since I neither can nor need to ask what kind or species of entity my own reality is, the interrogation seems to suggest that what I ask when I ask about my own reality is what it means to be real in the world. The phrase "in the world" only secondarily means my planetary location and environment; much more significantly it means my being already in a culture and tradition. This is exposed the moment I consider the question, for such consideration takes place only within a richly endowed language and history that allows me to give form and articulation to my reflection. It is this reliance on an historical and linguistic tradition that renders the model of a university classroom so fruitful: we are introduced to philosophy as an already established, ongoing concern that is both helpful and harmful, but necessary. Not only does this historical discipline offer us a wonderful vocabulary full of enlightening distinctions and analyses, it also offers instances of profound reasoning that we can adopt as our own. Insofar as the course may include some sense of the history of metaphysics, it also provides the ongoing refinement of argumentation. This last point can be used even here in the present inquiry, as if it were a class. The following is a sketch of a possible classroom curriculum.

The student is first offered the reasoning by Descartes. Ordinary, everyday language and experience seem to suggest that we think about ourselves as both body and soul, as when we deem a person morally good whose body is in bad shape. Descartes suggests that body and soul are both substances; when asked what substance means, we are offered the example of the ball of wax: since it is obvious the solid lump and the spread of warm liquid, though different in every empirically derived resource of learning about it, is still wax, the reasoning seems compelling. The changes are sensed, but the reality underlying these properties (or accidents) is known directly by the mind: the latter is called substance, the former accidents (or properties). The term "substance" hence means that which persists though the changes, and hence must be known only by the soul, which itself is then identified as a substance. That Descartes uses a physical entity, wax, as the model for all substances, including spiritual ones, may unsettle the student, for it shows the deep mechanistic spirit behind Descartes' dualism. Yet, the argument as such has immense power; and the student soon learns that even Kant, who seriously criticizes Descartes in almost every way, *accepts* the analysis of what substance means, except for the final step. The ball-of-wax argument, Kant argues, is valid; but it does not show that the external entity, substance, is known as an object by our minds, but is provided by the mind as a category for interpreting our experience. Whatever is experienced is guided by the categories that precede experience, but without experience these categories have no independent validity at all.

The student realizes a profound shift: the external as real cannot be known—indeed, it cannot even be imagined. What we call the external world— the world of possible experience—is therefore not real, but appearance. At first the student may think this demotes our external awareness to illusions; with this reading a new impetus is found for scepticism and cultural relativism: maybe "our" categories differ from those of other traditions. Loyalty to the Kantian text, however soon reveals that the sceptical and relativistic dangers are not consistent with the argument. Not only are these categories necessarily universal since they are, if Kant is right, grounded in pure logical forms, but the term 'appearance' does not demote the authority of math and science but promotes them: illusion has nothing to do with phenomena or appearances. Rather, it is the false doctrine that the categories of substance and causality are metaphysical that burdens science with excess baggage it cannot endure. Leave notions such as God, soul, and even ultimate reality out of science, and it will be free to do its own legitimate work unimpeded. What though, is now meant by reality? If space, time, cause, and substance cannot be applied to it, are we not left with mystical appeals or private revelations, marooning reality from any authority and enlightenment from reason? Kant argues that reason, unencumbered by experience, allows the regulative principles, especially in morals, to provide a noncognitive metaphysics. Freedom requires a suspension of the causal regress but is demanded by reason itself. So the real is morally significant: as a cause I am appearance, but as an agent, I am real. Unlike Descartes', Kant's account is not a metaphysical dualism, it is merely a transcendental one, presenting us with two different ways of thinking, not two distinct kinds of entities.

Two ways of thinking may be less vulnerable than two kinds of entities. The Kantian critique did not put an end to philosophical thinking, but provoked it to higher and further questioning. The student notes a further shift, enabled by Kant but demanding further thinking: A new term became metaphysically central by Kant's distinction: will. Will is not an object of experience, hence it is not appearance; the will itself is real; perhaps the will is the sole or at least ultimate metaphysical topic. Kant himself seems to suggest this, vaguely and indirectly; but Schopenhauer was more bold: will is reality and reality is will. We note the absence of the article; the primacy of the noun shifts to the primacy of the verb: it is not that I "have" a will; rather I *will*, and this willing is the metaphysically real. But it is not only my will, but the world will that emerges. Schopenhauer argues for example, that it is not the hand that explains grasping, it is grasping that explains the hand—and grasping is a mere externalization of will as reality. This revision is historically powerful, for it suggests that what it means to grasp is more fundamental than the grasping entity—a new way of doing philosophy is enabled by what we now might call the existential inversion; a development far more significant than Schopenhauer's own system.

The student now realizes the need for profundity in his own thinking; but he still needs guidance. How is it even possible to understand metaphysics—the study of reality—if meaning is somehow prior to thing or entity? The final text for the courses is Heidegger's popular little book, *An Introduction to Metaphysics*; and it is with his vocabulary that the fundamental term shifts again: it is not thing or reality, not substance or will, not consciousness or agency, but being—not being as an entity but quite simply the meaning of being, directly considered. The German phrase "Sinn von Sein" was used by Nietzsche in *Thus Spoke Zarathustra*, and is usually translated "the meaning of existence." The same term in Heidegger's work may be rendered in terms of the question: what does it mean to be: "die Frage nach dim Sinn von Sein." This question thus becomes a candidate for the ultimate metaphysical one, demanding as all genuine philosophical contributions do, serious reflection. If nothing else, Heidegger has shown it is possible to carry out actual, existential inquiry in which meaning is directly thinkable and not merely added on subjectively to some entity. What Heidegger, at least in his earlier works, calls 'ontology'—the study of being—when carried out in an existential way, thus provides for him the ultimate as a fundamental discipline; hence it is, formally, metaphysics. This seems to replace reality with being, indeed the instinctive primacy of the real begins to fade; if what it means to be is the ultimate question, then why even ask about reality any more?

The meaning of reality cannot be so easily displaced. The student in the curriculum just sketched has witnessed a series of fundamental transformations about how reality should be thought; he is not ready to abandon the term altogether, nor need he, for at least he can ask what it means to be real. With the help of Kant and Heidegger, he no longer relies on his earlier instinct to equate reality with external entities. From Kant he recognizes we often appeal to reality as the counter to appearance, for unless we distinguish between what is learned by means of the categories linked to empirical intuitions from what is learned directly as our own reality, we can never escape causal reduction, achieve completeness in our discovering, nor be free. But reality cannot merely be the opposite or counter to what appears, for at best that is a negative account. Three other characteristics of what reality means that have both historical precedent and a resonance with ordinary usage suggest themselves: (1) the real is the ground of the true; (2) the real enables thinkability; (3) the real is the ultimate.

1. If there is truth it is being real that makes it so. Even on the propositional level the reality of the rain is the ground of making the claim it is raining as true. This seems so obvious it is often overlooked as a resource when inverted: if there is truth there must be reality; or more specifically, if there is a specific instance of truth, the real must also be assumed as a part of that specificity. Thus, if an existential, moral, or aesthetic judgment can be true or false, then reality itself must be conceived in such a way as to enable such judgments. If our reflections on what it means to be provide truth or falsity, then such meaning, as true, is grounded in the real.

2. It is possible to imagine nonexistent things; this offers no threat since, as imagined there is no need to ascribe truth to them; we may falsely believe that some of the things we imagine do indeed exist when in fact they do not; this is simply error. To suggest thinkability is enabled by our reality means rather that being real is thinkable (in an authoritative way) in terms of what it *means* to be real. This may seem little more than to equate meaning with thinkability: the meaning of reality is the thinkability of reality. This suggestion is not as acarpous as it may seem, for thinkability is therefore grounded in *being* real; indeed what it *means* to be real is precisely that being real can be thought about; and it can be thought just because it *is* thought. To suggest that one can think meaningfully about the nonreal is to equate thinking with opining or imagining. Furthermore, to suggest thinkability is enabled by reality means that to think reveals our own being real as finitely both clear and opaque. Who am I such that I do *not* know myself—as least to the extent that I am sufficiently confused about my reality that I need to think about it? I seek, in other words, not only to understand myself as real but equally to understand why I am as real, yet mysterious. My self-ignorance is equally as wondrous and puzzling as my self-knowledge.

3. Metaphysics has long been identified as the ultimate discipline. When early atomists attempted to explain everything in one reductionist account, the appeal was made to the atom as ultimate: that which, in explaining absolutely everything either was self-evident (or self-explained) or it was inferentially presupposed as necessary but was itself inexplicable. Modern atomists argue exactly the same thing without realizing the reductio ad absurdum inherent in their account. Sophomores in high school ask of the theist: if God created all things, who created God? Transcendentalist thinkers such as Kant argue that because I do *in fact* think I must *be able* to think, and this enablement in terms of faculties must be available to us, so that the ways of thinking are ultimate. By saying they are ultimate we must, in some sense, recognize they—or the consciousness in which they reside—are real. To be ultimate is thus to be real; but also, to be real is to be ultimate. Metaphysics is *about* ultimacy.

Armed with these three ways of recognizing or identifying reality, the student is prepared to recognize his own being real as the ground of truth, enabling thinkability, and ultimacy; but only if such thinking avoids solipsism or relativism. This realization focuses his attention on the way to raise the question: what does it mean to be real? So when he reads through the first chapter in Heidegger's *Introduction to Metaphysics* he spots what at first may seem a purely social remark to ease a hesitant student. To the question (often spurred by reluctant parents) "What can I do with a philosophy major?" Heidegger suggests a reverse: ask rather "What can philosophy do to (or "with") us?" It sounds a rather neat riposte, a way of putting the onus on the philistine who rejects any learning that is not economically productive. It may seem rather general: any erudition in the arts and humanities refines who we are, opening up precious discoveries about our existence. The student may realize such studies are worthy in themselves; and this awareness may remove his hesitation to adopt a curriculum that refines him rather than one that promises easier affluence. Yet if the student is willing to let the suggestion develop, he may sense that perhaps Heidegger means something far more profound by the notion of philosophy *doing* something to us. Perhaps, in other words, Heidegger suggests philosophy can transform us, metaphysically. The title of his book, after all, is an *Introduction to Metaphysics*. In what way does this academic discipline offer the possibility of changing us so fundamentally that it is no longer a mere refinement of our learning, but a metaphysical transformation? Could it be that the study of metaphysics becomes itself a metaphysical event? If this were so, our comprehension of the transformation would be realized only by doing metaphysics itself. Ultimacy, grounding truth, and enabling thinkability would thus be impossible without being transformed *by* grounding, enabling, and being ultimate.

Perhaps vaguely—or perhaps not at all if the instructor is doctrinaire or the student unwilling—the undergraduate begins to realize that he not only discovers the ground by this deep thinking, but is the ground himself; he not only enables thinking but thinking enables him; he not only studies the ultimate but he is himself ultimate. These qualities are not latent powers that are merely discovered by doing metaphysics, they are accomplished, and as such they transform him fundamentally—that is, metaphysically. The final paper is returned to him, and he glows with satisfaction at the *A* he received; yet he notes there are still many marginal criticisms. This time, however, with his final grade secure, he reads the criticisms as part of his on-going, restless search: refinements are made that appeal to him; he learns more in part because he wants to learn more. He knows he has changed in a basic way, because there is now order, authority, and even joy in being the curator of his own reality. That his professor reads his essay on such a high level reveals to the student that he, too, is now in the historical stream: he can philosophize just because his arguments, though perhaps sound enough, still need refinement.

Refinement toward what? Greater clarity? Greater orthodoxy? Better thinking? Or perhaps, enabled now to grasp his own reality as worthy and capable
of thought, his reality is transformed. To be, such that what it *means* to be
is enabled *by* being, is not a mere discovery of what is the case: it is an assisted
accomplishment of altered reality. Thinking and being are, at this level, not
two distinct notions, for what it means to think is now revealed as a way to
be, and conversely what it means to be is forcefully revealed as a way to think.
    It may seem that the nature of this thinking is mere reflection, as I
might reflect on last night's dinner, or perhaps more helpfully, as I might
reflect upon the syntax of a sentence I have written or on the logical labels
I may append to a series of steps I have made in an argument. Reflection
itself is a wondrous phenomenon, and thinkers as important as Kant are quite
happily prepared to designate metaphysical judgments as reflective. There are
two reasons: one is that the term suggests such actions alone avail access to
the operations of our mind or consciousness; the other is, as reflective, they
presuppose an already existing mental phenomenon or state. Thus I can reflect
upon what it means to be angry because I remember once having been angry
at an earlier time, or I can enjoy a work of art at the same time as I reflect
on how this enjoyment differs from that taken in simple satisfactions of needs
or wants. How reflection itself is possible is beyond both the range and need
of this study; it is enough merely to point out in what way metaphysical
reflection is so entirely unlike all other species that it almost transcends the
range of the term. Metaphysics is indeed reflection, but only in the one case
in which what is reflected upon itself participates actively in the phenomenon.
It is not my being real as reflector alone that enables metaphysics, but my
being real as *actively* opening up so as to be reflected. My being real cannot
be a merely look inward at a nonactive entity. Both reflecting and being
reflected on are of a reciprocity that, because reflector and reflected upon as
two dimensions of the same reality are both *active*, requires transformation.
My being real is not a mute, passive object studied by an active consciousness,
nor is it a passive consciousness being pelted by signals from an active reality.
Thinking about our reality requires more than a mere mental act of reflection;
it also requires a metaphysical act that uncovers: the reflecting voyeur confronts the exhibitionist reflected—we must denude as we study, as if an artist
were, looking in a mirror, to paint his own undressing as a nude self-portrait.
It is because this reality must actively manifest itself for metaphysical reflection
that it must be understood as a transformation. This activity of being, however, is metaphysical, and cannot occur except as a way of doing metaphysics.
    The denuding act of being self-reflected is, as has been noted, not an
act of a subject, but of a being already and still in and with (the world),
requiring an inheritance and a personal history along with others; yet it
cannot be accounted for merely by historical, sociological, or psychological
phenomena. Our own temporal development, however, with its ebbs of es-

trangement and risings of belonging, requires a tidal telling, a story that waxes and wanes as days dawn and fade, else it would not be transformational. There is a protomodel of metaphysics in an earlier erudition of our being real, as we are transformed from innocence to responsibility. Before we can reflect as metaphysicians on our own reality enabling itself to be reflected on, we must consider the metaphysical nature of our earlier transformation from child to adult.

EIGHT

The Child

The fifteen-year-old, accused of a singularly heinous crime, sat on the edge of his cot, and wept bitterly on hearing he would be tried as an adult. The young guard, alone with him in the prison room, put his arm around the boy to comfort him. This gesture proceeded to intimacy. Caught in their dereliction, the boy stated truthfully he had not only given eager consent, but had initiated what to him was already a familiarity. The judge pointed out the law does not recognize underage consent, for a fifteen-year-old is not deemed capable of comprehending the full meaning of his act. The guard protested that the court already was trying him as an adult. How can one treat the boy offender as an adult and maintain the same boy, as victim, to be a child? The judge rightly dismissed this question as specious and irrelevant to the illegality of the guard's act; as a consequence, the guard was charged with the commission of a felony.

It is surely right of the judge, in this fictional case, to dismiss the argument; but philosophical thinkers are unfortunately not allowed that privilege. For this little sketch burns like a laser on the dark turmoil of the unconsidered. With the seeming proliferation of children committing terrible crimes, and the curious contortion of the law enabling prosecutors and judges to wave protective statutes for juveniles, what is offered here as a fictional fantasy may well be true enough. Such an event may actually occur. It is not, however, the sociological fact that matters here, nor even the propriety of the laws; what matters is what the sketch reveals about the murky vagueness concerning a necessary but rarely considered metaphysical question: What does it mean for there to be children?

The word *child* in its technical, dictionary sense means a human offspring who has not yet reached puberty; and it is in this sense that we usually think of innocence as well as the lack of full use or understanding of reason.

In ordinary discourse, the term also refers to our offspring of any age, as when we speak of our children, even when they are adults. There is a third sense, often replaced by the vernacular "kids," by which we mean any boy or girl not yet of legal age; indeed the terms "boy" and "girl" are very often used in this somewhat inexact sense, intending a postpubescent still short of full adulthood, as we might say "he's still just a boy" when referring to the fifteen-year-old miscreant. The legal term for such a person is "juvenile," which includes but is not restricted to that special agonizing period of transition called adolescence. In asking what it means for there to be children, I include all of these uses, taking the term in its broadest application; this broader usage is neither wanton nor arbitrary, for the term "child" bears with it a special sense of vulnerability that evokes a need for protection and learning that is applicable to all preadults.

To ask what it means for there to be children opens an entire battalion of other questions ranging from the troubling possibility of responsibility being partial, to the legitimacy of moral education. It even evokes the great question asked by Plato's Meno: Can virtue be taught? But these entirely worthy questions can themselves be deepened by the existential formulation. We may step back from these familiar issues, suspend briefly our eagerness to solve, and ask just what it is that lurks, hitherto unasked, in the *wonder*. We wonder what it means for there to be children. This formulation does not ask for definitions or rules of conduct or pedagogy, nor does it rest upon sociological data nor the status of social laws. It does not ask for the psychological or religious makeup of a child, but simply how we think about children already in the world. The last three words—in the world—require that we consider children as we find them, concretely and not abstractly. That the inquiry must begin within our culture does not render these reflections lacking in universality or authority any more than the need to discuss the issue in a particular language invalidates the legitimacy of the asking as a way to truth. To ask what it means for there to be children at all raises not only the metaphysical status of the child but also of the adult, and what it means for a culture to be a precondition for both.

The sketch of the same child as criminal and victim must not be derailed by offering speculative, social solutions. It may well be argued that the practice of ever trying any juvenile as an adult is simply wrong, precisely because the paradox of treating the same person as adult and child must be avoided. Such an argument may remove the legal mechanisms that make the paradox stand out, but does not remove the paradox itself. Both the inclination to adopt laws protecting juvenile offenders from the full harshness of adult penalties and the inclination to punish severely those of any age who perpetrate horrific offences remain even if the legal machinery is removed. Great wisdom can be learned in the struggle with a genuine paradox, but this wisdom can be purloined by banal resolutions that satisfy only the itch to remain untroubled. If the paradox emerges more clearly with the aid of legal language, its usage should be celebrated rather than lamented. But if the inquiry should not be derailed by speculative answers, its paradoxic impact requires that robust considerations of the underlying problems be articulated in existentially concrete terms.

It is the paradox that gives rise to the existential formulation. We ask what it means for there to be children because this is the question that provokes wonder at the phenomenon. The provocation, as paradox, need not be elicited solely by such grim situations as the sketch provides. Most children are not criminals, and most are not victimized by sexual abuse. Our first sentiment toward them may well be protective affection or even love; yet even as we love them *as* children we endeavor, by all the glowing efforts of concern and care, to transform them from children into responsible adults. Is this simply instinct? We teach them to wash, feed, and cloth themselves, to speak and read, to follow the basic maxims of civility, all of which prepare them for adulthood. We do these things even if we wish, especially in moments of aching charm, that they could, as Christopher Robin says, "remain six for ever and ever." Are children, because we teach them anything, only to be seen as not-yet adults? Or, as we ache with their looming departure, are adults simply outgrown children, cheated by learning and age, of innocence?

The use of the two terms, learning and age, that rob us of childhood may give us pause. Is sheer aging—that, is, growing up—enough? Simply for the boy to have lived three more years legally changes statutory rape to consensual intimacy: if we wait long enough, the paradox vanishes, overnight. This is a stark transformation, even if a legal fiction. The law again can serve as a lens: there is a crime at the other end of the scale. A child who is fed, clothed, and sheltered, but who is never taught anything at all; who is deprived of any fondness, denied any friends or playmates, and is not spoken to by her parents, has almost no language skills because no one ever talks to her, is deemed a victim of neglect, and neglect can also be a felony. By this law we seem to realize that simply growing, as a natural life form, is not enough. It is a further curiosity of law that the sadly unsocialized youngster on reaching her eighteenth birthday may still be deemed an adult; apparently she can give consent and be held accountable. There are, however, statutes that protect the socially enfeebled, in which, rather than treating the child as adult, the adult can be treated as a child. Again the paradoxes mushroom. It is not only her natural age, but her erudition and guided experience that enables true adulthood; and this erudition can be enforced by law. The great majority of parents, however, do not need such a law: it seems almost an entirely natural instinct not only to provide for the physical needs for the child to live and grow, but for the spiritual, cultural, and psychological needs to develop a certain minimal sophistication in what makes life worth living. This erudition, once formalized into law, becomes a right, enabling us to say the child has a right to a cultural education. Indeed it is surely a species of child abuse to deny moral instruction, allowing the child to "decide for himself" what is moral. Yet the child as precious also seems to have a "right" not to be cheated of its childhood. There will always be children; but sadly there is not always childhood, for many children are cheated of their childhood. If we see childhood as a paradigm of transformation, care must be taken to ensure that the worth of a child as child is not entirely lost in the ongoing effort to lead the child to adulthood. It is only when we recognize the worth of child as child that we can learn what it means for it to be transformed to an adult.

It may be helpful to return briefly to the image of the fifteen-year-old accused of a heinous crime who initiates intimacy with the guard. Even with our realization of the boy's possible guilt, the guard's impropriety disturbs us on at least four levels of violation: (1) innocence (2) vulnerability (3) learning (4) beauty. We do not like to see innocence abused, nor do we feel comfortable about advantage taken of the vulnerable; learning achieved through the coarsening of the young seems worse than learning deprived or delayed; and finally the natural beauty of the young seems too precious merely to gratify the lust of another. Each of these four demands analysis.

1. Innocence has two distinct meanings. On the one hand the term is entirely forensic and negative; it means: not legally guilty. A jury may believe the adult defendant actually committed the crime, but during the discussion in the jury room the members may unanimously agree that the prosecution simply did not make the case beyond a reasonable doubt, and so the decision is reluctantly made of "not guilty"; he is, as we are tirelessly told, "innocent until proven guilty." On the other hand, we also mean by innocence a state or condition that is not entirely forfeit even if illegal acts are shown to have been committed. This positive, nonlegal sense of the term suggests a playful, merry, unburdened delight simply in being alive and young. The lack of years seems accoutered with a lack of worries. A child who laughs cheerfully while at play is a thing of wonder; we sense, perhaps in a way that is warped a bit by nostalgia, that the purity and intensity of such unsmothered delight is enviable; no adult in the highest bliss seems comparable to the sweet totality of this unstrained, bubbling enthusiasm; even though few adults would ever become a child again. Often the purity of this delight is seen in the absence of the more bitter experiences that come later, that may cast a pall over the delights of age. Innocence in the first sense refers to actions (or nonactions); in the second, it refers to a condition or way of being; and precisely because it is a way of being it is considered unlosable or unmovable. The child as child is naturally innocent—not because of a lack of knowledge or experience, but simply because, as fresh, these experiences are pleasures just in being learned. What bothers us about the young guard includes his violation of the boy's innocence inherent in being young, even if the boy is also guilty.

We can imagine refinements to the story that makes this apparent violation more troublesome. The fifteen-year-old, with his erudition in the curriculum of the alley, may have been sexually active for some time, earning money in the oldest profession, enjoying it purely as a fleeting pleasure, entirely without shame or guilt. The young guard may have been an apprentice, and a virgin, working in a juvenile detention center for noble reasons, and coupled with the terrible arrogance of idealism, may have felt comforting and supportive in sharing this unexpected closeness; these factors may seem to confuse the labels: which is truly innocent? Perhaps a wise judge may ease the sentence against the foolish rather than evil guard; but the labels cannot be switched. The laws about consent are made to protect those innocent because of their youth, which is to say that in some very real sense innocence belongs to youth, and the guard's arrogant and naïve idealism notwithstanding, that innocence is violated. Naïveté is not innocence; the guard should have known better. If we care about this species of innocence, these laws may be justified, because innocence matters.

2. The young are not only innocent in this existential sense, they are also vulnerable. As young they have not yet developed the skills of defense; they are not only vulnerable to the lures of adult cunning, they are also vulnerable to their own torments. They have not yet learned the tricks of self-anesthesia—they do not know how to staunch the hemorrhaging from their wounds or how to avoid the self-inflicted barbs of unwarranted shame, guilt, and confusion. Some children manifest this vulnerability so palpably in their sweet faces they seem to carry signs around their necks: hurt me. It is the vulnerability of children that evokes in a majority of civilized adults a strong sense of protection. Driving near a school-yard where children are at play, instinctively we slow down, sharpen our wits and eyes for the errant ball that rolls out into the street, for children in their happy eagerness do not always look at the traffic. Not only is it easy to seduce a child, the consequences are terrible; the trauma may impede a healthy growth and cause greater pain than would be endured by an older victim. The vulnerability of the child and the seeming natural instinct of the adult to protect are abused by the guard's molestation; so that even if we refine the scenario to reveal the boy's delinquency and the guard's naïveté, we resist the appeal to soften our censure just because, *as* child, the vulnerability matters.

3. As powerful as innocence and vulnerability may be in influencing our reaction to the abuse, the effect on the boy's learning may be the most telling and persistent. This outrage against learning has three manifestations: (a) the damage wrought to the boy's ability to learn *at all*; (b) the coarsening of his learning; (c) and the putative message or content of the learning. With regard to the first point, children learn in part because of trust; they also learn in part

because they are eager to do so. The abuse of a child may shatter both trust and eagerness, so that they learn not to learn. For some, this learning not to learn may result in a retreat into a permanent childishness, as the victim holds on to the shattered remnants of the only safe cocoon it knows. For others, it may induce a rejection of childhood altogether, in which the victim becomes streetwise beyond his years, assuming an adultlike assurance purchased by the harsh initiation of the cruel discovery that others are there solely to be used or conned, as he was. In either response, the effect is the same: learning, as opposed to mere experiencing, is either abandoned altogether or enabled only by prodigies of courage on the child's part and prodigies of ingenuity on a teacher's part. We consider such impediments to learning as outrages. (The possibility that prodigies of courage and ingenuity may overcome the dire injury of abuse provides a key to understanding the difference between learning and experience. To learn is to be guided toward an understanding supported by culture of one's own worth, which, when grasped, also reveals the worth and meaning of others; to experience is to acquaint oneself without moral guidance to the tactics of prudence and advantage as one discovers empirically what happens in the world.) The loss or even diminution of the will to learn is so dreadful that it is deemed a usurpation of an inherent right: children ought not to be so abused.

Second, the need for, and perhaps even the persisting delight taken in, learning, may be so robust that even when outraged it may continue in another, though vulgar, form. This may be called the coarsening of learning. On the casual level, this means we learn to read but read trash; to see plays, but only cheap and tawdry ones; to amuse ourselves, but only in the grossest satisfaction; to earn collegiate degrees, but only to add to our pockets; we learn the propriety of conduct, but not self-refinement; we learn to appreciate the contributions of others, but ascribe to them merely base motives. If these qualities seem generalist and vague, a more concrete example may show us the true danger inherent in the education of vulgarity. Parents may assume an indifference if their children read trash or cheat on exams to get into law school, but when their offspring attend segregated "private schools" that inculcate racial hatred, or join up in so-called religious cults where secrecy, terror, sexual abuse, and slavelike intimidation turn them to zombies, alarm ensues. In some school districts it is the parents themselves who matriculate their young into institutions that provide little more than racist propaganda, establishing a weird camaraderie of putative superiority based on skin color and the techniques for guerilla terror against the despised. Cults, on the other hand, alarm most parents as well, often leaving a species of kidnaping and enforced "reprogramming" as the only tactic to offset the influence. These two underworld institutions are probably much rarer than the alarmist press may lead us to believe; they deserve our reflection here as vivid reminders we do indeed fear—indeed fear greatly—the coarsening of education; and this fear inescapably demonstrates that moral education is both possible and matters greatly. Meno's question, "Can virtue be teachable?" is here not so much answered as assumed—*vice* can certainly be taught, else we would not fear the two vulgar institutions. To vulgarize learning is to dismiss or diminish the idea of intrinsic worth, and judge our human effort as grounded only in inherited and arbitrary values. On this erudition the greatest wisdom is deemed to be disdain for universality and truth; the greatest virtue is distrust in anything noble—this is mislabeled "honesty"; it entails a certain delight in depicting ourselves as foul and obscene, in order not to be gulled by those who suggest excellence.

Finally, the coarsening of learning itself also effects its contents and messages. What we coarsely learn are the facts and the evidence that support nihilism, and with it the exaltation of one's own gratification coupled with the glee taken in exposing the sham of solicitude. When the curricular diet consists solely of the menu from the fast-food chains of academic drive-throughs, the ensuing ill-health is inevitable. To feed the learner only with base foods distorts the healthy view of what a child is, and such a diet is itself abuse.

4. We shudder at the image of the child's intimacy with his would-be protector in part because of its violation of beauty. "Beauty for use too rich," Romeo says at his first glance at the fourteen-year-old Juliet, manifesting the sense of awe at something so lovely it should not be "used." That Romeo also feels erotic longing does not detract from this reverential sense bestowed on a vision of fresh radiance that is so often felt at the sight of a child. Most children are beautiful in precisely this sense of nonutilitarian appreciation. Children, of course, especially the very young, need to be cuddled, kissed, embraced, and held; but only a pederast would confuse this with violational abuse, for the violation is a use of beauty, and as such defiles it, making the use ugly. This unique beauty is a species of purity; we see it in the perfect smoothness of the skin, the brightness of the eye, the red of the lips, the length of the lashes, the glow of health. . . .

But wait. So might we look at the rose. Is this not a danger: the child does not delight in his own beauty; only we, the adults do. Is it not unseemly that the sheer delight we take at the visual presence of children may tend to distort how we think about them and hence how we are ought to treat them? A case can be made, for example, that the latter decades of the nineteenth and the first of the twentieth centuries, especially in England, stretched childhood beyond its natural tenure to the disadvantage of the entire society. Stories such as *Peter Pan* by James Barrie (1902), with its emphasis on never growing up, and the more horrific *Picture of Dorian Gray* by Oscar Wilde (1891), in which the adulation of youth is presented as the justification for grotesque crimes may be seen to adumbrate the contemporary television fare of depicting most adults as stupid, venal, and sexually pathetic; whereas children are fonts of wisdom, natural goodness, and innocently successful in sexual play. Indeed, the huge variation in the ages of consent in other nations contrasts with the tendency to extend childhood in the English-speaking world. Is not the adulation of youthful beauty and innocence a distortion that itself may be unhealthy?

Dangers of excess exist in every worthy phenomenon; to recognize it here is thus not remarkable. The beauty of children is a rather special case, however, for it emphasizes the priority of the existential formulation: what it means for there to be children asks in a way that forces us to confront not only what children are, but also what it means to be adults in a world where children are, and in which their beauty becomes a special problem.

It is not only their beauty but their linkage to our own existence that troubles us. Although most of us can recall many exquisite moments in our childhood, as well as a few horrific ones, which may or may not be distorted by the selectivity of memory, it remains difficult for adults to realize they once were children *as* children and not children as seen or remembered. Watching them at play or trembling in seeming groundless tears and fears at times may seem akin to watching aliens from another planet: how is it possible to comprehend being a child? Jaded by our own faults and failures, can we even remember our innocence? Can such total dependence on others ever be envied? The child may be our origin, but it is a mysterious one; indeed it is even a misleading one. The more we look to children as an explanation of who we are, the less revealing the reflection becomes. This curious cleavage from our natural beginnings is itself an oddity, for it would seem the influence of our childhood should be so great that memory would constantly remind us of such profound discoveries. As I write this sentence, however, I cannot remember learning any of the words I now use; nor can I recall learning to tie my shoes or use a fork or how to button my shirt; all of which are supremely important things in everyday life. It is almost as if the very forgetting of innocence outranks remembering it—as if memory as forgetting constitutes part of that essential transformation by severing the links between our childhood and adulthood. Can it be that the phenomenon of transformation is necessarily violent in the sense of rebellion against the hegemony of our origin in others and our origin in ourselves?

One of the most painful and wrenching phenomena of this transformation provides a few clues. Adolescence, like paying taxes and dying, is a necessary but agonizing inevitability, even as it occasions moments of sublime self-discovery. Manic/depression or bipolarity is usually thought a disease, but in adolescents it seems a normal condition; they swing from joyous ecstasy to moping ennui, suicidal risks, and fake adventuring. Much of the agonizing is caused by changes in the body of course: a girl's first period can be terrifying or satisfying, a boy's voice changing can embarrass, fascination with the opposite sex may seem to unhinge our interests in all else; even as a sublime disinterest in the other gender follows in the next hour. Yet these physical changes often pale in comparison to changes in our consciousness and even ethical balance. As the adolescent seeks by natural maturing to achieve a painful but necessary independence, the transformation of our physical reality requires a corresponding transformation of our thinking. Who we are seems to depend less on our secure place in the family and more on our own developing sense of responsibility. Established norms become first irritating encroachments on our new independence; yet when violated, they seem to achieve a new level of sacrosanctity; this teetering annoys not only the parents but the adolescent. What he or she seeks is some sense of self that is consistent with his or her new independence and vulnerability. If the achievement of this new sense of self may for some seem to necessitate a rejection of familiar values, the danger is that all values will seem arbitrary, which is precisely what the emerging adult fears most. These phenomena are familiar enough, and if the tortured, joyous adolescent has had good training, a sense of humor coupled with continued trust in the love of family and friends usually helps to mute the rebellion to an acceptable, if frustrating, species of learning. Not all are fortunate; war often deprives the young of both childhood and adolescence, as do natural calamities and moral outrages. Even in such cases where social violence replaces the more private wrenchings, the transformation still occurs; innocence must be replaced with a maturer sense of wonder.

Adolescent transformation consists in an awareness of the metaphysical enablement of being oneself. Of this dreadful transition it is often said that the teen has no real sense of self; in fact, it is exactly the opposite: it is the confrontation of oneself as real that transforms. Confronting the reality of self, however confusing, must, by its very nature, be formidable, as is the reality of courageous fear emerging from the simple instinct to run away from pain; the latter is merely a natural emotion that protects us from external danger, the former is existential awareness of fearing fear because we matter more than our safety. Transformational adolescence alters self-awareness from what to who one is; it sunders our mere belonging to what is our own, to enabling it. There is a paradox here: the more loving one's preadolescent familial existence, the stronger the teen is prepared to undergo the transformation; but the more loving the family, the harder it is to leave. Like all true existential transformation, in adolescence or in courage, the pretransformed state is not abandoned but developed. Once one has faced fear courageously, it is almost forgotten what it is like simply to fear—the courage or the cowardice remains after the transformation, making it difficult to fear simply as a spur to safety except in cases of sudden urgency. In exactly the same way, the adolescent glimpsing his true reality can never retreat to the preadolescent staging of being oneself without any troubling awareness of what that being means.

A further point deserves brief reflection. Children are often designated as "our future." This may be a mere banal remark concerning our selfish concerns for old age: we want our grown children to take care of us, if need be. There is a far richer meaning to this phrase, however, that reveals a curiosity: we somehow care about the posthumous future, not in the sense of personal immortality, but simply in the realization that our own deaths do not eclipse our interest in what follows, even beyond the normal concern that those we love will live well after we die. This works in two ways: we want subsequent generations to benefit from the wealth of meaning our well-developed culture provides; but we also want the future generations to protect, preserve, an refine the culture itself. We think of children as our inheritors; to think this way requires the supreme importance of cultural education. This reflection, however, is often self-transforming: to be able to share our culture with the young, we must also develop our own refinement and hence greater enjoyment of our own cultural learning; but it is the truth inherent in our culture that matters, else there would not be learning, but only indoctrination. Educating children in the glories of Mozart and Shakespeare not only refines their sensibilities so that their capacity for richer enjoyment is possible, it also enables a deeper appreciation of the great truths about human existence that are discovered in the artworks of our canon. We consider a world bereft of such art to be less worthy and less truth revealing; thus it matters that such learning takes place. Neither can we be indifferent toward a future in which moral and ethical notions are lost: we do not want our grandchildren or great-grandchildren to return to the barbarisms of slaveholding, dueling, or human sacrifice; so we teach our young to see that such things are wrong. For there to be children allows us to think meaningfully about the distant future in a way that matters. History has sadly revealed that some generations do indeed regress, that new advocates of ancient savagery can persuade us to relinquish what is precious; the extent to which such regression is either caused or at least abetted by our failure to teach well burdens us with a heightened sense of duty. The reality of children as learners enables this realization: it is part of what it means for there to be children. They learn, and in learning they are transformed from innocence to maturity.

If the essence of a child is innocence, the most revealing manifestation of this is in their playing. Children play. Indeed, in their early years, play seems not only the prerogative but their innate destiny. They seem to know how to play as if inspired by a divine gift akin to genius; they do it so well. Creating their own magical worlds they can become entirely absorbed in their fantasy. Especially when a child is alone, playing on the kitchen floor with utensils, or outside on the grass with pebbles and sticks, they seem masters of their universe, entirely unrestrained in their imagination; being innocent, their free imagination suffices. This skill at self-amusement appears a native inheritance rather than an acquisition, a freedom bestowed on them simply because they are children—a freedom lost as innocence is transformed. Adults play, too; but for them it is an achieved delight, the product of an effort to disengage from the practical; freighted with rules and strictures, mixed with other matters—the need to be victorious, recreated, or ennobled—not pure as is the child's. Yet, adult play, as art, may be our highest achievement. Is there any freedom quite as pure as that found in a child at play? Or is it an impropriety of diction to call it freedom at all? If there is no restraint upon the child's imagination, and if the child seems to play spontaneously, then why not call it freedom? It may not be the freedom of the postadolescent who recognizes first his rights, and then his responsibility; but it is at the very least an unfettered use of his imagination that brings pleasure, and that seems to qualify at least minimally, for lack of restraint is a legitimate usage given to the word *free*, as when we set free the prisoner by unshackling the irons from his ankles.

Is the child truly free? Do adults truly play? Here is the essence of the paradox: being free and playing seem entirely different when applied to adults and children; yet the reluctance to dismiss their univocity altogether is as telling as the need to distinguish. Perhaps nothing is more clearly transformational than the paradoxical shift of sameness of these two notions: there is nothing more natural than for a child, and nothing less natural for an adult, than to play; nothing more burdensome for an adult, and nothing more unburdened for a child, to be free. We lose too much if we "solve" the problem by defining the two terms in two different ways. How did it ever happen that we designate the telling effort and sacrificial energy of a pianist as *playing* the piano? Surely that is hard work, not play. We call a performed drama a play—what is playful about *King Lear*? The child bursts with an explosion of joyous energy, and we say he is free; the same person, years later, is burdened by a terrible oath or solemn promise that torments him, and we say he is, as responsible, free. Being free makes the adult unfree. What it means for there to be children is thus a paradox: once lost, innocence is not only gone forever, it is profoundly forgotten: we quite literally cannot recall what it means to be innocent; yet its past is part of our reality: we are now as once innocent—though it cannot be recalled, neither can it be dismissed. The paradox is an essential part of our being real. The transformation, over gliding swiftness of years, is metaphysical; it is also analogic to the paradoxical transformation of doing metaphysics: the premetaphysical as an analogue to innocence can never be regained, yet unlike the loss of innocence, it is not inevitable, but in some sense it is essential. However, the transformation from innocence to maturity and guilt surpasses mere analogy to that of metaphysical reflection; the former also enables the latter, as if metaphysical learning is the furtherance of learning to be an adult. It is tempting to suggest a species of dialectic, from innocence to guilt, and then from guilt to metaphysics; but since most of the world's population goes through the first stage, but apparently only the rarest of the rare accomplish the second, it seems unlikely that the development can be understood as a natural process of reasoning. Yet, the rarity of metaphysics itself must be scanned as a serious problem: perhaps a majority of civilly refined adults do indeed participate indirectly and randomly in self-critique; perhaps all of us have moments in which we wonder, in awe of truth. Perhaps. But if our loss of innocence is a paradox, so too is the rarity of metaphysics: in some sense it cannot be ordinary—though it must be universal. The occasional, brief insights most adults have of their own reality cannot truly be judged metaphysical, since the discipline by necessity requires sustained and critical effort. Those who doodle on a notepad while speaking on the telephone are not artists as we conceive Rembrandt as an artist; and those who on occasion shiver with the magnitude of their wonder when they look at stars or concentration camps are not philosophers as Kant is a philosopher. Difficulty in precisely assigning a label cannot, however, be allowed to derail the significance of the analogy: just as the transition from innocence to guilt is a metaphysical transformation, so too is the transition from premetaphysical to metaphysical wonder. How can we answer how many are transformed before we complete the asking of what it means to be transformed? That it can be done at all is what matters.

NINE

Conflict and Coherence

The transformation from innocence to responsibility offers an analogue to the transformation from responsible adult to metaphysician on at least three levels. The first is that as innocent the child is *not able* to be responsible, so the preinquirer is *not able* to think metaphysically. Whatever enables any personal activity is more fundamental than the action itself. The second level of analogy is that the transformations can be gradual and incremental or sudden and unexpected, though in neither case is the development explicable entirely by natural means. The third level is that in both cases the history or unfolding of the learning that transforms is itself a part of the transformation. The metaphysical transformation is not, however, a mere extension of the development from innocence to responsibility, for the point here is not to reduce the second to the first, but simply, by means of the analogy, to help us understand that in learning metaphysical truth we discover certain characteristics that may be more clearly illuminated by making the comparison. The question that now needs consideration is this: what is the *nature* of the metaphysical transformation wrought by learning metaphysics?

As real, we are the ground of truth. The "reality" of a rock, however, is also the ground of whatever true statements are made about the rock, so it may seem that being the "ground of truth" is not that significant. The truth about the rock, however, requires a thinker other than the rock. The truth of our own thinking is grounded in the reality of our thinking: there is no truth without a thinker, and when the reality of the thinker grounds the truth of the thinker it can do so only by becoming available to itself as truth. It is tempting to suggest that our awareness of being both real and a learner of the real is what matters, so that self-awareness—always a privileged phenomenon—is the learned transformation. This temptation must be resisted, for it is a mere recognition of a distinctive cognitive state: it is an epistemological rather than a metaphysical discovery. We are transformed not because we are aware of ourselves as real, but because our being real itself is transformed so as to enable self-awareness. What happens to us when we think about our being real transforms our reality and not merely our thinking about reality. It is also tempting to suggest that our thinking about our reality is somehow the cause of our transformation; this, too must be resisted, because it is backward: it is the transformation that causes, not the thinking that transforms. If we begin by noting the various ways we think, and then discover one way we think is to think about being real, we are forever locked into the prejudice of initiating inquiry solely from the perspective of cognition or consciousness, not of being real. There must be, then, something inherent in our being real that is more fundamental than our thinking about it, even though thinking may be a necessary condition for it to be the ground of truth. At the very least, our own being real enables our thinking about what it means to be real. In what way does our being real enable such thinking? Only by transformation. The suggestion is that were transformation of our reality not possible we could not think metaphysically; yet the converse is also true: unless we can think about our being real we cannot be transformed in this higher sense. The previous chapter shows an original transformation from innocence to responsibility; the second transformation is from responsibility to the intrinsic worth of the truth as grounded in our being real. The definite article in the last phrase is crucial: *the* specific—i.e., metaphysical—truth is grounded in our being real. There are many true sentences or true beliefs that abound in our experience of external nature; the present suggestion concerns only metaphysical truth; and the arguments seem to show that metaphysical truth is only of our own being real. The metaphysical truth of our own being real cannot, however, be understood as mere mind, or reason conceived as a faculty, and certainly not the awareness of facts. This point itself has important historical precedent. Socrates, for example, in Plato's *Phaedo*, rejects Anaxagorous' account of 'mind,' precisely because it was understood too narrowly.

The name Socrates offers a fulcrum for the Archimedean lever by which the world itself can be moved. In his *Apologia*, we learn his famous adage that the unexamined life is not worth living. A few initial remarks concerning this famous passage may prepare the way for a more profound analysis. Logically the claim does not entail the inference that the examined life is worth living: both could be worthless. Further, the claim is not that the unexamined is less worthy than the examined: it has no worth at all. This could mean either that examination is a necessary but not sufficient condition, or that it is both; so that what may give life worth is entirely and only its being examined. The adage itself further leaves unclear what qualifies as an examined life: does a one-time session with a guru, therapist, or priest render one's life "examined"? Or must the examination be ongoing and continuous? Furthermore, are all examinations equal? Suppose I examine my life but do so badly? Is my life worthy or worthless? Or is it simply less worthy? If the reader reflects not only on the single passage but considers the entire collection of dialogues, it seems some answers to these questions can provisionally be entertained: the examined is a life worth living; the examination is itself a part of the life of the examiner, hence must be ongoing; the examination must be philosophical, not merely psychological or even moral; not all philosophical examinations are equal. These refinements, however, are themselves the result of examination not only of the text, but of our own understanding. The very nature of such examination must include itself, requiring one to ask whether the adage is true. It does not take much reflection to see serious reservations about its veracity. We think of kind, saintly, self-sacrificing people who either by their natures or by their adherence to a religion may bring about great improvement in the world, but who do not examine themselves at all: do we dare suggest such lives are not worth living? One may consider the great artists who contribute so much to our appreciation of life and our wisdom as well, and hesitate to deny their lives were worthy. We also think of two young people deeply in love, joyous in their ecstasy—are their lives worthless? Given the saints and the artists, the lovers, the scientific discoverers, explorers, inventors and great lawmakers, some of whom may not have examined their lives, it would seem outrageous to accept the Socratic claim. The dangers multiply quickly: perhaps by widening what is meant by "examination," we can include any who contribute to the quality of our experiences, and hence avoid the seeming outrage. Or, we can consider the term "worth" in a clever way, admit the elitism, and say only philosophers have worthy lives but many others have "valuable" or "justifiable" lives. Either way, the boldness of the claim is sacrificed to make it palatable. At the very least we recognize that the three key terms, unexamined, life, and worth, must themselves be examined.

The context of the Socratic adage cannot be overlooked. He is defending his life as a philosopher on the charge that philosophy itself may be both impious and corruptive. But to whom is he directing his defense? The *polis* of Athens, and indeed the entire Greek society, had for centuries developed a culture of argumentation; the sophists thrived, the Athenian government was democratic, disputation was encouraged, clever eristics were celebrated, young men and boys were educated in part by watching brilliant debates among men famous for their dialectical skills. Even the great Pericles in his Funeral Oration recognized the love and enjoyment Greeks took in discourse for its own sake. Every Greek, but especially the gathered citizenry of Athens, was prepared to appreciate critique; so that when Socrates suggests to the assembly that the criticized life—the life most of them knew, at least indirectly—was not only worth living, but was a life identified as being Greek, his appeal had a patriotic quality. "You and I, as Greek, already know that critique is a virtue, a peculiarly *Greek* virtue; would you censure me for *that?*" It is sadly overlooked by many critics that this adage was not a shocking claim by a rebellious, lonely revolutionary, but an appeal to Athenian virtue—and indeed, given the closeness of the first vote, it showed some resonance among the populace. The paradox is, and remains, that philosophy as self-critique is both familiar and strange: it both challenges and reinforces piety; the Athenian assembly recognized the paradox. After all, they knew who Socrates was, and they knew what he was doing.

What was he doing? If Plato's dialogues are even close, we can elicit indications of how Socrates may have intended us to understand the adage. Especially in the so-called aporetic dialogues, formal definitions always fall short; the inquiry is restless; and near or at the end of the discourse, Socrates often claims that the inquirers are more uncertain after the discussion than they were at the beginning. Some scholars see in this an indication of genuine scepticism, but they do not take into account that learning one's naïve, original beliefs were inadequate is an epistemic gain, not a loss; furthermore these utterances about our ignorance do not diminish the implacable feeling that we have indeed learned much about courage from the *Laches*, temperance from *Charmides*, and love from the *Symposium*, that exceeds a mere awareness of our relative ignorance. Rather, what seems to emerge from reading these dialogues is that the various virtues as virtues include our continual thinking about what they mean, not because the inquiry fails, but because it succeeds—by making further inquiry more profound and exciting. If by "knowledge" we mean putting an end to our wonder, then perhaps we are required to recognize our ignorance and hence are "sceptical," but this is a glorious scepticism indeed, for it allows for genuine learning, and a deepening appreciation of the wondrous depths and richness that the topics deserve. When Socrates discusses piety with Euthyphro he himself is learning precisely because he is unsure whether there may be a tint of impiety in his own examinations; Euthyphro's actions may even be pious in some sense, but this youth is not willing to question or challenge his piety, so he lacks the spirit of genuine inquiry, hence must be lacking in piety since piety includes being critical; this lack alone is the ground for Socrates' disappointment. Is this, then, merely a confession of human finitude: we can learn more and more about the virtues, but as finite will never grasp all? Perhaps; but even the aporetic dialogues are truth revealing, and hence must be grounded in the real. The real, therefore, as the ground of the true, must itself admit of degrees, and this leads us directly to the remarkable view of reality behind all of Plato's inquiries: it is a participatory metaphysics. Parmenides seeks to convince us that individual things are illusions; they are not at all real. The atomists seek to convince us that all things are equally and completely real. Plato seeks to show us that both are wrong; particular entities are somewhat real, because they participate in the form, and because of this participatory metaphysics, knowledge of the real itself is participatory; yielding itself, in part and by degree, only to those who constantly inquire. Perhaps perfectly just states cannot be found in our experience, but relatively just states certainly can be, since Athens was more just than Persia, and the ability truthfully to rank one state as more just than the other is based on the reality of justice itself, even though our understanding of that reality is indirect.

Participatory metaphysics, with its introduction of degrees of being real, is not his only contribution to the problem of ultimacy. In the *Phaedo*, Socrates describes his youthful disappointment with Anaxogorous' account of mind (Nous): he had expected to be told, by this appeal to mind, what was best. Mind, in other words, should tell Socrates why it is best for him to be in prison rather than in exile. In the *Republic*, Socrates explains this more fully by pointing out that the form of all other forms is the good/beautiful. This puzzles the modern mind: what does good have to do with metaphysics? Surely the good is a value term, belonging in ethics rather than the study of reality. Do we explain this by claiming Socrates, unlike the majority of pre-Socratic cosmologists, was "interested" in the virtues, and thus linked his moral concerns with his metaphysical reflections? Such a suggestion overlooks the authority in his reasoning. Our own reality may be participatory, but it is still real and still ours; and how we think about our reality must entail the truth of participation: I can succeed or fail to certain degrees at being real, and hence goodness, as metaphysical success and badness as metaphysical failure, is not distinct from reality. To think about ourselves as real must include our success and failure: the sharp distinction between metaphysics and ethics is retrograde to wisdom. Certainly if the virtues are understood as constituting a life lived well, and if life lived well is more real than one lived badly, and if the virtues are virtues only as examined by wisdom, then the logic is obvious. If wisdom itself is a virtue, then truth itself—and the search for it—matter; so both participatory metaphysics and developmental or transformational refinement of our own reality seem to follow. The examined life enables the virtuous life, and worth becomes itself a metaphysical notion. The struggle for truth and hence worth is not a mere means to achieve, but participates in the enabling of, truth and worth. It is only if forms are falsely seen as entirely transcendent rather than enabling a participation that is itself a passionate struggle, that the antiphilosophical viruses of misology and scepticism, relativism and nihilism, threaten.

We catch a glimpse of this in Book V of the *Republic*, in which Socrates directs our attention to the second, rarer education given only to the would-be rulers. Among the already trained guardians, a very few who manifest a love of learning, the "philomathes," are selected to become philosophers; the nature of this exalted education is the development of a longing for truth for its own sake. The lover of beautiful things or persons must be self-consciously refined or transformed so as to recognize that the love of beauty itself, in which beautiful things participate, is what uplifts the learner to dialectic, or in the later image, to extricate oneself from the darkness of the cave. Such illumination or erudition is possible only for those already trained in a cultural tradition, and who are blessed with a passionate love of learning. The trek out of the cave is arduous and demanding, requiring the courage learned in the first school, but also the ceaseless longing of truth that is honed only in the second. In this way Socrates expands on the adage of his defense: the unexamined life is akin to the mere lovers of beautiful things who do not realize the possibility of loving beauty and truth in themselves, he claims that such people are like those asleep: what they see is a dream. Only those awake—those who love beauty itself—see reality.

However, what is truly promising in the Socratic adage is its inversion. Not only is the unexamined life not worth living, the "unlived" life is not worth examining. Unlived here means not living in a manner that enables examination: life as a mere biological duration in which simple gratification of wants and the procreation of offspring, followed by death, is not so much "lived" as endured. What Glaucon scorns as a mere state of pigs, which is the product of providing basic wants and needs, is recognized by Socrates as enabling no ground at all for justice, much less for the truth or beauty of justice to be loved. If there is no virtue possible in the pig state prior to the introduction of luxury, poetry, and spices, then neither can the examination of such a state provide us with truth. To be worthy is impossible without examination, but examination itself already requires some sense of being able to be worthy. It would seem, then, that examination is necessary but not sufficient for worth. To enable this paradox, the learning must be divided.

Socrates tells us of the two species of education: the education of the guardians that produces courage and loyalty to the state, and the rarer education of the ruler, that produces wisdom; the first is required of the second and to some extent enables it. Analogously the educational transformation from innocence to responsibility enables the rarer transformation of learning metaphysics by being metaphysical. In the first, we learn of ourselves that we are responsible for our actions; in the second we learn what it means to be the reality that both learns and is learned, enabling fundamental truth. I become morally worthwhile as agent by the first learning, and become metaphysically worthwhile by becoming more real through the second learning. In both cases being entails being worthy; but in the second learning I become the ground or basis of the truth being learned: I am real as true. The unexamined life is not worth living and the dull life is not worth being examined. That by which I examine life cannot be external to the life of the examiner, hence the need for the inversion. Even with this addendum, however, an impertinence of inquiry demands another consideration: is it not possible to examine badly? Surely there are some who examine life to their own detriment; they become wretched and unstable, either because they learn they are indeed unworthy, or because the method and manner of their inquiry is ill-conceived. Plato himself suggests this in the *Phaedo*: philosophical inquiry may lead us to frustration and hence misology. There are, apparently, those made less worthy by inquiry or examination. This reflection gives us pause. Do we amend the adage to read: only successful examination makes life worth living? Or: only those capable of proper inquiry—whatever that means—should examine themselves? Or is it rather: examination is risky, but the risk is worth it? The boldest suggestion is that the results of the inquiry are not what matters, but the inquiry itself: it alone bestows our worth. Just as moral responsibility enables us to be censured and praised, it is yet better to be free than unfree (innocent); so self-inquiry may be injurious, it is yet better to learn what it means to be real.

There is a nineteenth-century romanticism inherent in this last suggestion that reveals a darker paradox. Lessing, one of the fathers of this romanticism, in a mythical account is famously visited by God who offers with his right hand the boon of truth, and with his left the search for truth. True to his humanity, Lessing chooses the left, leaving truth itself for God alone. This is an attractive story up to a point, but what does it mean to love the truth, to search for it, but when offered it, to turn it down? How can we say we seek truth if we reject it? To say we seek the seeking of truth opens the way to the ridiculous: why not seek the seeking of the seeking? If offered happiness ought I reject it because the search for happiness is better? It means nothing to say I search for happiness if, on finding it, I reject it. Does Shakespeare keep from writing plays so as to enhance his desire to write plays? The Lessing story suggests a Platonic participation or perhaps even something akin to existential transformation: as human we must long or search for truth without ever possessing complete knowledge; but this longing does not entail a repudiation of partial possession: neither Plato nor Lessing argues that the search or love for truth implies either a rejection or an absence of truth altogether. We do participate in reality according to Plato, and hence are real enough to become more real. Lessing's denial is not a species of modesty or humility; it is rather based on the deepest metaphysical awareness: I cannot be offered fundamental truth since by definition for it to be fundamental truth it must be grounded in my own being real. God could offer an entire encyclopedia of factual knowledge that might benefit Lessing, but not truth itself. Why? If my own being real is the ground of metaphysical truth it may be necessary for it to unfold by developing stages of transformation, but for it to be given all at once would not transform Lessing, but simply replace him—render him divine; make him God; but being God he would not be Lessing.

Thus, a further discovery needs to be recognized. The search for my being real must be my search, it cannot be bestowed—though the cultural richness that enables me to search must be. My own being real is not only the ultimate topic of metaphysical inquiry, the inquiry itself is inherent in my being real, a role that cannot be assumed by anyone else; but as universal, it cannot be restricted to private feelings: as reasoner I think of myself in terms of universality. Just as my moral guilt cannot be transferred to another, neither can my metaphysical inquiry, since such inquiry is always of my being real. The mutual interdependence of my being real and my inquiry into being real now embraces a third: my becoming worthy of being self-examined is paradoxically in part, enabled by the examination itself, so that I become worthy of examination in part by examining. But if I cannot substitute another for the inquiry, it is also true that neither can I inquire solely on the basis of my being an isolated, particular entity; for what I inquire into is what it means for me to be real, and this "meaning" necessitates the world as that in which I already am, a world that already offers the long history of metaphysical inquiry, along with the rich abundance of artistic and scientific discovery—as well as contemporary co-inquirers who challenge, protest, and share. Meaning is found only through a special species of learning, so that we can be said continually and rarely to learn who we are in reality only when our reality is transformed by metaphysical truth.

Such learning is not thinking about thinking, but thinking about my being real as thinker. Since the first step of thinking is either to establish or discover coherence, the temptation may be to create some principle or scheme and apply it to a phenomenon—in this case the phenomenon of thinking—as we do with any other phenomena. This temptation must be resisted, for no scheme can precede being real; yet for our own being real to be thinkable it must, in some sense, either already be coherent or be transformed into coherence. Coherence is wrought in two ways: either with elements that are similar and different, or with forces that conflict. Any act of classification, such as sorting apples from oranges, is based on what is shared as common among apples as distinct from what is shared as common among oranges. This sameness and difference can be codified, and thus used as a rule or scheme. The purest form of such thinking as coherence is the classical Barbara syllogism, in which membership in classes provides the authority for the inference. But there is another, more dynamic species of coherence, and that is the conflict of opposition that creates union by violent authority. This latter coherence cannot be depicted with glib or idle examples, but two analogies can reveal how it is learned: counterpoint in music and irony in literature.

It is truly remarkable, in a way, that a simple ascending melodic theme can be enhanced by the simultaneous playing of the same notes in reverse descending order. Given any melody, the composer can enhance the sound in a multitude of ways: Playing it in thirds or octaves, for example; or providing a rolling rhythmic bass; or embellishments of other sorts. One can alter the dynamics, the keys—especially in shifting from major to minor—or even the volume. Yet the least intuitive, but often the most effective, is counterpoint. Indeed, the entire history of modern classical music seemed to avalanche in wondrous and complex scores once this technique was developed, especially in the emergence of the fugue. Yet, a fugue seems so odd, so counter-intuitive—but only when described: as listeners we do not find it counterintuitive at all—in fact it seems so obvious and wonderful as we hear it, we feel as if it were always meant to be. Counterpoint, however, is not merely an enhancement; it produces an independent musical event, having its own status. It is dynamic conflict that produces a new unity. Music, both historically and artistically, is transformed by counterpoint. Is it not, however, a mere peculiarity of western music that merely appeals to the ear and hence has no significance beyond the art form? Perhaps, but there is an isomorphism between counterpoint in music and one of the most troubling figures in literary art that suggests both conflictive forms may reveal more than mere aesthetic criticism.

It is perhaps fitting that irony itself ironically is so often misconceived and ineptly explained by texts. The pedagogue is often misled by the multiplicity of the forms it takes: the rather simple instance of Swiftian irony, which approaches sarcasm, is fairly easy to describe and even easier to exemplify, and so it is often used as a standard. However, the subtlety and depth of certain forms of what is misleadingly called tragic irony—for not all tragedies are ironic and not all instances of this species of irony are tragic—are so elusive and so exquisitely crafted they seem to escape ready recognition as a figure, leaving the reader or audience deeply moved or uneasy without realizing why. It is properly called a figure of speech, as are metaphors, similes, and analogies; yet it seems almost a "figure" of being real, as when we speak of perverse fate providing a curious fitness that is counterfitness, as we might say it is ironic that Beethoven's deafness kept him from actually hearing his own music. Furthermore, in art, even though we as an audience know full well that Juliet will soon waken does not stop us from agonizing with Romeo at her putative death. It is almost as if we know as audience but are ignorant as art participant, so that we know and not-know at the same time. The term "irony" is sometimes used entirely devoid of a literary figure, often as a substitute for fate in its role in actual human events that occur as mockeries to what seems fitting. Yet it is fundamentally a figure of art, if not only of speech; and as a figure it provides access to truth unavailable by any other way. Irony works—that is, it is an effective way of revealing truth and delighting audiences or readers—the question is why it works so well, and how it works at all. Like counterpoint, there is something counterintuitive about it: why should it be so satisfying to see the cruelty of fate mock what is ordinary fitness into a counterfitness? When Don Alvaro, in Verdi's *La Forza del Destino*, brings Leonora in disguise to his friend Don Carlo whom he has wounded, he unwittingly enables Carlo to kill his own sister. When Agave returns from the dark mountain triumphantly dragging the spy's body, she discovers to our horror he is her son. The most loyal Othello is beguiled into becoming the most disloyal husband. Terrible as these endings may be, the audience recognizes their dramatic inevitability, and hence "fitness." Even the comic Touchstone in *As You Like It* tells us: the truest poetry is the most feigning. These ironies in art are all the more effective for their being merely one way of achieving fitness: when Florestan is released from his prison and the wicked Pizarro is punished, the finale to Beethoven's opera, *Fidelio*, is deemed as nonironically fitting—it is right and enormously satisfying. When Rosalind brings all the lovers together for the great communal marriage at the end of *As You Like It*, nothing could be more fitting: indeed, it seems the essence of what fitness should mean. Even some tragic works are nonironic: Macbeth and Richard III both deserve to die. In these cases we say it is fitting not only because it satisfies, but because the triumph of good over evil is a great resolution. If we contrast such fitting with the darker counterfitting of irony, a certain unease or even discomfort accompanies the judgment. How can it be ironically fitting? In both species of art, the term "fitting" is understood as an aesthetic coherence: the plot unfolds in a way that seems somehow inevitable; the finale seems governed by dramatic acceptability. But in the ironic art, what is "fitting" is achieved by thwarting what is usually fitting: a very strong passion within us aches for a coherence that fits our expectation: when this is violated the normal reaction is to reject it or dismiss it, or even to turn away from it in disgust or revulsion. When the violation is artful in its irony, however, a new and hitherto unrealized potency is released: we are able, somehow, to accept a deeper sense of fitness that is rooted in our essence as finite, fated beings. This cannot be accounted for by mere appeals to the realization that life is unfair (which is an unsavory fact, hence, true) or even that lack of success does not forfeit our worth (which is a discovery of what matters, hence is true). The point is rather that these ironic endings enable a truth that is neither fact nor value: a truth based on what it means to be real.

At this point, however, these reflections no longer can be mere analogies. Irony is revealed as metaphysically significant. As a way of thinking about our own being real, the figure of irony becomes the metaphysical transformation found in paradox. Paradox is to metaphysical thinking as irony is to literary art. What enables the truth of the latter is the reality of the former. We are, as real inquirers into our being real, paradoxic. This is not a mere shallow appeal to the inscrutable mysteries of a highly complex psychology, for a problem—and all complexities are problems—is not a paradox: the former is in principle, solvable; the latter is not solvable, but can be truth availing. Indeed were paradox solvable it would not be a source of truth. Our being real is thinkable only as paradoxic; we ourselves are, therefore, as the ground of such truth, paradoxic—but what avails us of such thinking is enabled by our being transformed. Access to our own being real is enabled only by a species of thinking that is violent; this violence as paradoxic must be turned on thinking itself; but since metaphysical thinking concerns the truth of our own being real, it is also necessary for our reality to enable and ground the violence as a species of coherence. What happens to us when we think metaphysically is that we become the basis or origin—the enablers—of our own paradoxical essence.

The analogy with dramatic irony is helpful here: the delight we take in the coherence of morally justified triumph is nonviolent, precisely because the story justifies our gratification of how things ought to be. When the tragic drama violates these expectations, we are forced by the genius of the artist to find a violent coherence, the coherence revealed by the ironic figure. In a similar way, the coherence that renders a puzzle solved or a question answered is nonviolent; but when truth happens as paradoxic, the coherent reality is achieved only in paradox, and this would not be possible unless we ourselves as real were fundamentally changed or transformed. We are transformed into enablers of our own paradoxic essence. The nature of the paradox is that metaphysical inquiry provokes deeper asking and newer wonders rather than mere answers that satisfy, so that curiously our ability to ask triumphs over our ability to answer. This must be carefully examined: we learn that metaphysical truth itself is found in profound inquiry or asking, not in any set of terminating answers. (Hence, Socrates' continual insistence that at the end of the dialogues we are more "confused" than at the beginning. He does not mean we have learned nothing in the dialogue; quite to the contrary, the learning is profound just because it enables a newer level of asking.) There are indeed answers in abundance if the inquiry is thoughtful, and some of the answers may even be terminal in the sense we now know something we did not know before. But the deeper discoveries are of paradoxic truth and hence paradoxic reality, meaning that inherent in the profound are forces that seem almost inconsistent, though the depth of wonder allows us to see them as conflictive rather than self-contradictory. To enable the shift from seeming irrational to productive conflict, as irony and paradox obviously do, our own reality itself must be transformed. Only with the realization are we able to understand the paradoxic/ironic nature of that transformation: we are led to become the basis of our own paradoxical being. Were we not to do metaphysics we would not be paradoxic in our meaning. We learn that truth is in the asking, not only in the answering.

In the year 2000 I published *The Asking Mystery*, in which the argument is made that asking is both more profound and even more thinkable (or even rational) than answering. One must distinguish ordinary from extraordinary asking: the former always requires the projection of a scheme—as a calendar is a scheme that enables asking what day it is. The latter however has no scheme: that enables fundamental or metaphysical asking is not a scheme but our own reality—indeed not our reality conceived as an entity that exists, but reality as that which anchors meaning. Fundamental asking is therefore the basis of metaphysics; it outranks any theoretical answers (which must always be schemes) because, on the ultimate level, it alone enables them. Fundamental asking must be restricted to the meaning of being real. As Kant argues in the *Critique of Pure Reason*, the fundamental enterprise of metaphysics must be the isolation and identification of the faculties that allow us to do those things that characterize us as rational beings: math, science, morality, and art. The German *vermögen*—faculty—means that which makes something possible; it is an enabler. (This is why Heidegger argues that Kant is actually carrying out a fundamental ontology.) Two things about this reading of Kant are significant: first, the ultimately real is our consciousness; the various ways of being conscious are the faculties; they are enablers of what we do as thinkers. Second, the ultimate form of the faculty enablers is asking about what it means to be as enablers: what does it mean to be as scientist, moralist, artist, or even thinker? Kant's distinction between noumena and phenomena, which seem so upsetting to his critics, is demanded once we realize what makes rational activities possible are the metaphysical bases that gives them meaning: the enablers. These enablers are simply ways of our being real as conscious. We cannot ask what day it is without first assuming or imagining a scheme like a calendar; we cannot ask about our thinking without realizing what enables us to think. The latter are nonschemed, hence real, and because they are real they cannot be thought by means of the faculties themselves—thus what is learned by means of the faculties is distinct from the reality learned by considering what makes the activities of consciousness possible.

In the book on asking, the subtle but supreme importance of the distinction between two senses of the possible is highlighted. In the first sense, the possible is a purely formal notion allowing us to entertain anything at all that is not self-contradictory, as we might entertain the possibility of red oceans or honest politicians. This is distinguished from possibility in the sense provided by modal logic that whatever actually exists must also be possible. Here, possibility is within the actual, or even the real, so that all actual snowstorms are also possible snowstorms. To reach into the actual to see its possibility as the basis of asking, and if we ask about being real we also must ask about the possibility inherent in it, and this possibility is the ultimate origin of fundamental asking. When we shift from being real to the possibility of being real we address the very askability of metaphysics; the askability of being real paradoxically—i.e., as conflictive—confronts the possibility within the real, and this possibility is accomplished by a transformation from the real as actual to the real as possible, and thus can take place only as a species of learning, indeed a learning that is violent—either ironic or paradoxic.

The final dialogic sketch in the opening chapter shows the dramatic enablement of learning by the actress playing Portia and by Portia herself learning what she becomes in loving Bassanio. For both, the learning is wrought by a transformation that violently extracts what it means to be as ground or enabler of their reality. In Chapter Six, Lincoln was probed as a paradoxic, hence violent, learner by enabling the truth of a nation's essence to emerge by enabling not only its actuality but its possibility. Both of these educational models suggest that asking itself, if done profoundly, is a resource of truth; that is, we do not merely ask for the truth, the asking itself enables the truth—there is truth already in the asking. In philosophical inquiry there is even more truth in fundamental asking than there is in any theoretical answer. But, to go beyond the original argument, if there is truth in asking, and truth is grounded in the real, then there must be reality in asking, so that asking is the availability of meaning—what it means to be real. To be able to do this requires that we be transformed. After all, in the opening sketch the youth realizes he is afraid to leave and afraid to stay; his is a paradoxic conflict. By asking what it means to fear conflictively, he enables his own being courageous.

TEN

Origins

In Plato's *Republic*, Socrates provides a mythical depiction of learning, in which the student is violently transformed by his painful exodus from the cave. The dialogue makes it clear that true education must be distinguished from mere indoctrination, in that the former has its genesis from within. Even though our own power to think is in some sense already in our souls, lying dormant as it were, educational violence is needful before we can be transformed into being able to uncover truth. Earlier in the dialogue, in his depiction of the divided line, Socrates identifies dialectic as that by which we transform ourselves to learn our reality. The term 'dialectic' is itself troubling, but it is clearly an active, discursive, and disputational species of critical reasoning that alone provides us with metaphysical learning, not by spotting some external entity or even theoretical construct, but by enabling us to become our own resource of universality and authority. The story of the painful trek outside the cave is clearly meant to show that philosophy does not merely provide us with new information, but that we must be so fundamentally changed by our own journey that we are alienated from the way we were before the trek. In Book V, Socrates uses the metaphor of sleeping and waking to account for this transformational erudition: lovers of mere beautiful things are like those asleep, lovers of beauty itself are like those awake. Philosophical education is the harsh awakening. To be awakened is to be transformed from dwelling in illusion to dwelling in reality; this wakening is not merely the recognition of the true state of the world about me, but of my own reality, for it is I who sleep and wake, so the fundamental difference is my own being. True education is the noise that wakes us up. Why "waking"?

In Shakespeare's *Richard II*, the king returns from his Irish wars to find his realm in dire rebellion. At first he despairs at the reports, but Aumerle, somewhat harshly, says, "Comfort my liege; remember who you are." Richard then responds, "I had forgot myself: Am I not king?/Awake, thou sluggard majesty! Thou sleep'st." Act 3, Scene 2. Such waking is metaphorical, but it represents what Socrates intends: premetaphysical thinking is premetaphysical being. To learn to think philosophically is to learn to be a philosopher, as Richard first fails, then succeeds, however briefly, at being king, by realizing—being awakened to—who he is. Socrates identifies the species of thinking that wakes us up, and thereby enables our being real, as dialectic—the only access we have to forms such as good in itself or justice in itself. It is tempting to understand dialectic as merely critical—that is, as refutational. In most of the aporetic dialogues, a discussion about a virtue is initiated with what is apparently a rather naïve definition that is then proven false; but even subsequent refinements turn out to be vulnerable to critique, leaving Socrates and the other interlocutors as "more confused than before," so that the dialogues appear to be exercises in futility. This sense of refutation, however, cannot provide us with truth or reality, and is certainly inconsistent with the lofty role given dialectic in the analogy of the divided line. I should like to suggest, therefore, that the earlier suggestions are critiqued not because they are false, but because they are true. They are attacked not in order to *dismiss* them, but to torture them to reveal their secrets. Laches suggests courage is staying at one's post, Charmides suggests that sophrosone is civil and gentlemanly behavoir, Euthyphro identifies piety as pleasing the gods. Traditionally these suggestions have been dismissed as failing as definitions owing to their narrowness or vagueness, but most of the dialogues themselves fail to achieve a definition. What matters, then, is not so much whether the interlocutors in the dialogues find a terminating answer but that the readers of the dialogues participate in the fundamental act of learning, as audiences do of dramas. Hence it is the inquiry itself that is philosophical, not the answers. It is an inquiry absorbed by the reader in such a way as to wake him up; to give the reader a terminating definition allows him to go back to sleep.

The myth of the cave may well be the finest exemplar of metaphysical transformation, providing a sense of what happens to us when we do metaphysics. It is thus one of the origins for this inquiry. However, most of the argumentation in the *Republic* is analogic or metaphoric. A more modern thinker who yet provides a similar learning is Kant. Between the first and second editions of his mighty *Critique of Pure Reason*, Kant wrote The *Prolegomena to Any Future Metaphysics*, ostensibly to provide a less daunting outline of his thinking to wider audiences. In this tantalizing work, however, Kant suggests something only implied in the two editions of the *Critique*: Future metaphysics—that is, metaphysics as a "science"—must consist solely of a critique of the faculties. Such a critique, however, is nothing other than a study of what enables us to do those things that identify us a rational people. In the cognitive realm, I first am able to receive information about the external world (empirical intuitions) or about how I perceive the forms of these intuitions (pure intuitions), and this ability is called sensibility. Sensibility is thus nothing other than receptivity: to be conscious I must be able to receive. I am then further able to connect empirical intuitions with authority, and this ability is called understanding; finally I am able to generate and follow laws, an ability called reason. I can also add to cognitive consciousness other faculties that enable me to think with authority about my actions, such as the will, and can even spot the imagination as a faculty applicable not only to cognition but also to art. In all of these cases the enablers of these cognitive, moral, or aesthetic acts lie in us. To carry out a critique of these powers requires no other resource save our own conscious reality; hence if the future metaphysics is to be possible it must be grounded in ourselves as real. Since for Kant, the existence of anything can be known only by empirical intuitions connected by the laws of the understanding, it is impossible to know directly anything that exists that is not the object of possible experience. Thus the existence of such things as souls, freedom, God, or even the universe, is not knowable; however, the *reality* of our own being can be *thought* in a lawlike way, so that existence as an occurrence in the world of experience is sharply distinguished from reality, which is rendered thinkable only by what Kant calls regulative (as opposed to constitutive) principles. If a critique of the faculties is the only way to do metaphysics, our own being real—and not our being entities, substances, or things—alone can account for what enables us to do rational things such as making judgments in mathematics, science, morality, and aesthetics. That the origin of these fundamental grounds of rational activity lies within us rather than in the world Kant calls a Copernican Revolution, i.e., a fundamental transformation of what enables truth. It is a transformation achieved by self-realization: as one consciousness I am able both to become the basis of the authority that provides the moral, universal law, and to discover the principles within myself that account for making sense of the natural order in the world of experience. It is this ability to realize I am the same one reality that thinks in both moral and scientific ways that brings about a reason-generated conflict reflected in the antinomies. A critique of the faculties is apparently rich enough not only to recognize that unanchored metaphysics is bound to be confounded, but even to glimpse the resolution: though I am still one consciousness I must distinguish phenomena or appearance from noumena or intelligible reality.

Unlike Plato, Kant does not provide a transformational metaphysics, for the Copernican Revolution is a transformation in the history of thought, not in the metaphysical status of the thinker. Yet his contribution may be even greater, for he has identified that which enables us to do rational activities to be more fundamental than the activities themselves, and more important, more fundamental—and hence "real"—than the *products* of these acts. The possible within the actual is thus spotted as being real. My body, with its sense organs, may *exist;* my rational activities, which may require nonempirical grounds, may *occur* as events; but only what *enables* such occurrence should be called *real*, for the critical study of such faculties or enablers is the only way metaphysics is possible, and metaphysics is the study of the real.

There are some difficulties with this account, not the least of which is Kant's appeal to what he calls a metaphysics of morals. Perhaps this phrase refers to the simple critique of the faculty the makes morality possible, the will. The will, however, is not a cognitive faculty—it does not provide knowledge; rather it provides an account of one species of events (human actions) that is not dependent on the understanding, especially causality as a sequence. Reason, reflecting on its own nature as law giver can generate the categorical imperative as the supreme law of moral conduct; but adherence or nonadherence to this law cannot be explained solely by reference to the law itself, so an independent faculty, will, must be assumed. What seems inevitable then is that the faculty of willing does not enable cognition, but responsibility, and hence is no longer mere appearance. Is, then, the will itself real? Are noumena real? Is the unknowable thing-in-itself real? Perhaps; but even if we assume them to be real, they are not, strictly, the object of metaphysics, for that now-altered discipline is entirely critical: it concerns itself only with a critique of the faculties—that is, it is a critique of our own inherent *abilities* to do those activities that mark us as thinkers. We are once again the ultimate resource for truth.

If Kant is the second resource for this inquiry, the third is Heidegger. In his later works, Heidegger abandoned the term "metaphysics" because of its being constantly misinterpreted, but in his early works, what he calls the Ontological Difference is the capital distinction behind his thinking. The distinction is between 'being' conceived as an entity and 'being' conceived infinitivally as the ground of meaning, so that the question What kind of entity is the mind? is now transformed to What does it mean *to be* a mind? or even more simply What does it mean to think? Unlike Kant's "Copernican Revolution," which refers to the actual historical discovery of the method of critique, the Ontological Difference is more akin to Plato's transformational account of the educational exodus from the cave: it is ongoing, torturous and alienating from the comfort of uncritical, everyday existence. What Heidegger in *Being and Time* calls inauthentic existence is a constant lure, lurking even in the higher accomplishments of our endeavors, and indeed cannot ever be entirely transcended. Yet, to question what it means to be *(Sinn von Sein)* is also always there, lurking as a possibility even in the most mundane.

Heidegger's insertion of the term "meaning" as a necessary part of what he calls the fundamental inquiry carries with it both dangers and strengths that have undeniable influences on subsequent thinkers. One of the dangers is the tendency to see truth as perspectival in some sense. As early as *Being and Time* (1927), the reader cannot escape this impact in his terminology: he identifies, in this book, his method as hermeneutic or "interpretive" phenomenology; he accounts for what he calls Understanding as 'the projection of possibilities'; he also speaks of the 'overcoming' *(Überwindung)* of traditional metaphysics. As an instance of this last, he published in 1929 an original, stunning reading of Kant's *Critique of Pure Reason* as an *Auseinandersetzung,* which means 'dispute' or 'argument' in ordinary German, but which Heidegger understands as a deliberate attempt to shake up or to do violence to an original text in order to allow its deeper truth to emerge. The *Critique* was thus interpreted as laying the ground for fundamental ontology. In the essay "The Origin of the Artwork" (1935) he points out the pivotal significance of what he calls the "preserver" (that is, what we would call the "appreciator"), ranking him above the artist. These passages—and there are many others—place the reader or interpreter as central to a metaphysics defined with the term 'meaning'; and as a consequence there developed a vast and influential movement that spread far beyond philosophers to include other disciplines, especially literary critics, known as deconstructionism. For many, though by no means all, deconstructionism has come to mean a species of cultural or personal relativism, in which the term "truth" no longer has what is now designated as "foundationalist" or nonrelativist status, but is radically perspectival. Heidegger is not a relativist, nor indeed are all deconstructionists; but this movement is important precisely because it brings to focus a special problem inherent in claims about meaning. Though deconstructionism is a broadly conceived movement, one of its central tenets is to define 'text' not as the words written on a page, but as a phenomenon or event that entails the reader as interpreter. Hence there is no external entity, the Cleopatra in Shakespeare's play, but only the Cleopatra that emerges in the phenomenon of reading or performing the drama. This occasions a multiplicity of texts, not only in the sense of different readers but also in the sense of there being subtexts and metatexts and other levels of text that seem to multiply like taxes. There is a serious legitimacy, however, to the underlying problem; but it is not one that originates in deconstruction itself, but has been with us from ancient times. Is there only one way to play Cleopatra? Of course not. But to admit different actresses may enrich our appreciation of the drama in different ways does not entail that all renderings are equally valid or even equally true. Some are better than others. This seeming threat to traditional or foundational truth is not, however, restricted to literature, nor even to art in the broader sense. Even in the strict mathematical sciences, such as physics and chemistry, interprative judgments must still be made. There is a fact: a piece of iron placed near a magnet will be attracted to it. We say this is true. Yet we also realize that there are profound disputes about the nature of magnetism and even the nature of the mathematics that in part accounts for our understanding of it; yet few scientists deny that there is magnetism, or that we know something of how it works. Science itself is a history of hypotheses, which on occasion turn out to be verified: it is no longer a hypothesis that the earth is a spherical orb; it is a fact. It is thus wrong to say that hypotheses can only be falsified; Ptolemy's geocentric hypothesis was falsified, Copernicus's heliocentric hypothesis was verified; for it is now a fact that we can circle the earth in spaceships. Among interpretations, whether scientific hypotheses or renderings of Cleopatra or of our own phenomenological existence, it does not follow that the notion of truth must be debased to that of opinion. Neither should the uncertainty of our knowledge be allowed to serve as an argument for the relativity of truth, an error that itself is based on supreme arrogance, as if unless I know something it cannot be true. As thinkers we approach philosophical truth as nonarbitrary, without having to put it into a proposition that can be verified or falsified. There is, therefore, no need to disjoin the foundationalist aspect of Heidegger's thought from his interpretive analysis of existential phenomena.

The necessary insertion of the term "meaning" into what Heidegger calls the fundamental question—What does it mean to be?—thus has dangers, though they are avoidable. Yet the insertion also has advantages; for if the fundamental discipline *requires* the term "meaning" the harsh disjunction between fact and value, itself an enemy to thought and truth, must be avoided. It is this particular advantage that provides support for metaphysics as transformation. If meaning is an essential part of the fundamental discipline, to engage in the latter may well affect the former. This is part of the reason Heidegger insists on the "violence" inherent in thinking. It is perhaps unfortunate that some critics insist that the violent transformation inherent in fundamental ontology reflects Heidegger's brief but regrettable association with the Nazi party in 1933, offering a moral version of *modus tollens*: if Heidegger's thoughts led him to support the party, and the party must be morally rejected, then we must reject his thinking. This glib misuse of the rules of inference is another instance of the dangers of vagueness in reading Heidegger. There is no reason to see the need for metaphysical violence solely in terms of a particular political violence; indeed to suggest it is to fly in the face of the texts themselves. The point here is both far more legitimate and far more serious. Something like violence is necessary if philosophical thinking transforms the thinker; but if this is so, a metaphysical inquiry must, if it is to be true, enable such violence. The inclusion of the word *meaning* into the very definition of the fundamental discipline does not render it relativistic as some deconstructivists suggest, but it does render it dynamic, so that truth matters. It is chiefly for this reason that Heidegger must be seen as one of the three sources or origins for the present reflection on metaphysics as transformational, along with Kant and Plato.

It is surprising in a way that Heidegger is so harsh with Plato, for he shares so much with the Greek master. According to Plato, we can approach an understanding of justice itself—the form of justice—by ranking the various participants, so that realizing a timocratic state or man is more just than a democratic state or man enables us to have some sense of what justice itself means; for Heidegger what it means to talk is possible only by recognizing inauthentic talk as distinct from authentic talk. So both thinkers recognize some sense of success or failure as essential for doing metaphysics. Thus it is not merely the centrality of our own reality that grounds our possibility to do metaphysics, but the further notion of truth being made available by the conflict of success and failure, waking or sleeping, authentic or inauthentic. These tensions are always with us and within us; without them metaphysical thinking would not be possible.

In the later Heidegger the growing importance of language becomes a dominant theme, at times almost seeming to outrank being itself—another similarity to Plato. Language reveals its proper nature not in the proposition, or even in the analysis of syntax or use, but in its remarkable ability for figures, especially in poetry. Heidegger is very specific about this: poetic language reveals metaphysical truth in a way not available to any other human activity. Figures such as irony not only add aesthetic refinement to literary works, they echo a deep though imprecise sense of our own dramatic essence. Heidegger's oft-quoted remark that language is the house of Being itself is a metaphor, but its metaphysical profundity depends upon the figure; we are linguistic beings in our essence. Here, too, there is an analogue with Plato, for in the *Republic* Socrates assures us that the state built by words is more real than any state we discover through experience: word is truer than deed—at least in philosophical matters.

In the opening chapter of this inquiry, each of the sketches designed to show what transformation means turns on a single word; the term "courage" transforms how the youth thinks of his fear and the term "loyalty" transforms how the jury thinks of the defendant's actions. This is an artifice, of course— not every transformation needs be occasioned by a single word—but the device serves to focus attention on the realization that metaphysical truth is grounded in our own reality as speakers and listeners.

It is not, however, what Heidegger says about language that is his only resource; it is also how he speaks and writes. One of the most popular of his publications is the relatively short work, *Introduction to Metaphysics*, the opening chapter of which is a remarkable philosophical *event*. With great literary skill Heidegger speaks of raising the question of Being. It is a haunting, reverent appeal to the listeners or readers to sensitize us to the lure of the question itself. It has an almost "intuitive" overtone, suggesting that metaphysics is far more than a mere discipline within the academy, but a pervading question that persists in the unfolding patterns of our existence, enticing a rarity in thought itself; yet at the same time it has great authority, showing remarkable erudition and philosophical sophistication. This very artistry, however, irritates the unsympathetic precisely because it is so esoteric. Yet its author succeeds in revealing what it means to ask metaphysical questions, transforming us as we read it. Can it be that philosophy, the most critical of disciplines, requires a sense of reverence at one's own ability to ask what it means to be? And if so, can that reverence be wrought by a literary *style*? Why not? If Heidegger's point is that a certain truth lies hidden in the camouflage of everyday discourse and hence everyday analysis, then an unusual appeal to the reader or audience that such truth is there in our own being may be necessary to evoke in us a certain sensitivity to our ability to confront it. If accessability to this truth is blocked by banality, the very originality of his language may be required. The opening sentence, Why are there things rather than nothing?, serves as a heuristic shock to transform us into enablers of fundamentality. Rather quickly we learn that the opening salvo of his questioning itself is reformed into the more familiar terminology Heidegger gives us elsewhere: we must ask about the Being of beings.

It is fundamentality itself that lies at the basis of Heidegger's major contribution, and this notion must be duly considered. There are disciplines and ways of inquiring; some are more basic than others. Logic, for example, has a purely formal precedence; basic grammar, however, may in some senses precede even logic, for unless there are rules that allow us to speak properly, we could not discover the formal rules of inference. These two disciplines may rank formally, but since both are *merely* formal, we recognize that already we are making distinctions that apply to the ranking, suggesting other ways of thinking. Why, though, rank at all? Insofar as there are various disciplines, ways of thinking, topics, questions, and realms, any self-reflection at all requires some sense of what is derived from what, which are necessary for others to be possible, what is fundamental. These last three words give us pause. What is being asked by them? Fundamental has both positive and negative significance: negatively it means there is no other prior or earlier presuppositional basis that must be assumed; positively it means that as basic all other procedures or inquiries proceed from it; it is the origin of all else. What then, is the fundamental discipline? Whatever the fundamental discipline is, it must also account for the very questioning about it, and the only inquiry that seems to be able to do that is, for Heidegger, metaphysics—or to be more exact, that species of metaphysics that he calls fundamental ontology: asking about what it means to be. It is the *ability* to ask such a question that Heidegger seeks to provoke by the language he uses to "raise the question" of Being. Later in the work, in the section "Thinking and Being," he spells this out with greater precision by his analysis of *noein* as more fundamental than *legein* and *phusis*, and his lamentation that *legein* has been emasculated by the modernist rendering of it as "technique." What is going on in the opening chapter may well be understood as species of *noein*; but in any event, the reader has been alerted to a remarkable power lying within us. We can ask about Being.

But what ranks Being above reality? Are these selections arbitrary? Kant says reality is the realm of metaphysics, Heidegger says Being is. Which is correct? Plato says the forms are ultimate; from Aristotle, through Descartes to Berkeley, substance reigned, until Hume dismisses the term as meaningless. The entire history of philosophy may seem, if scanned casually, as a dispute about ultimate terminology: from Thales to Anaxogoras it was 'world' or 'things'; for Plato, forms; from Aristotle to Hume, substance; for Kant it is reality; for Heidegger, Being—though Heidegger revisits the pre-Socratics and claims they also were talking about Being, but were misunderstood. Are these differences serious? Perhaps they were all talking about the same thing, using different words. Perhaps this short list of candidates should be seen as progress, the later the better. Perhaps the selection is arbitrary. Such a historical sketch may seem trivial unless it is seen as a way to focus on the shift from Kant's 'reality' to Heidegger's 'Being'; the former is patently oppositional, i.e., real as *opposed* to appearance so that metaphysics, if it is possible, cannot use the categories of the understanding; the latter is also in some sense oppositional—Being as opposed to beings—but more important, if it is to be thought, it requires the insertion of the word *meaning*.

It is the insertion of 'meaning' *(Sinn)* that provides our transformation. To learn to be able to inquire into what it means to be is itself a metaphysical transformation, and what makes it transformational is its inherent fundamentality. Just as the innocent child is metaphysically transformed because as child he is *unable* to be responsible, but by education is enabled to be responsible, so the premetaphysical adult is unable philosophically to inquire into his own fundamentality, but by metaphysical educational learning is able to do so. Since, as Plato, Kant, and Heidegger argue, the ultimately real is our own reality or being, to be able to learn what this means requires a fundamental transformation.

Yet this spotting of three historical origins would merely be eclectic support unless what is borrowed from them is not merely their doctrines but their reasoning. We are not only able to reason, we are also able to learn how to reason about our reasoning, to think about our thinking, and even—to exist in such a way as to render the meaning of existence available as truth. This can only be possible if doing metaphysics transforms us metaphysically.

Throughout this inquiry emphasis has been placed on the metaphysical nature of the transformation. It is neither a physical nor a psychological alteration, not a religious conversion nor a theory adopted as an ideology; it need not change our personality nor our habits. It may seem, then, a phantom, or a purely formal notion that has no consequence. Yet such a sterile reading is inappropriate: to deny the transformation is physical, psychological or spiritual is to resist reduction to these disciplines; it does not entail a complete sequestration of our passion. Plato uses eros both as a metaphor for and as a condition of philosophical inquiry; Kant speaks of the reason-based need for the motivational phenomenon of respect; Heidegger speaks of authentic existence as care. If metaphysics is fundamental in the positive and not merely in the negative sense, then there would have to be manifestations of the original transformation in the more familiar hues of who we are. It is for this reason that the opening chapter of this inquiry provides five dialogic sketches that rely on such phenomena as fear, awe, reverence, and appreciation; but it is wonder, discussed in the second chapter, that seems the key philosophical passion. The search for philosophical truth may bear with it many emotional responses; it may produce a sense of loneliness: aching to share the richness, the thinker finds few if any capable of participating. On the plus side, on the rare occasions when another does share, the attachment can become exquisite. Along with other lofty enterprises, philosophical seeking enables us to spend time with the noblest minds and spirits of our history—not just philosophers but poets, dramatists, scientists, and historians. Even idle hours become resourceful, as waiting for the bus or at the checkout lane may occasion musing on great thoughts, which is a delight. Yet the constant frustration of the restless sometimes causes moments of misology and despair. Such reactions are not universal, since some of them may rely on a distinctive character, but they are not entirely trivial, for they show in part what it may be like to reflect metaphysically. If there is to be a special, revealing passion or feeling, however, it cannot be among such responses, for what in sought here is the felt awareness—if there is any—of being transformed.

Caution here is of singular rank. "I used to believe X, but now I believe non-X" is not an argument or even a reason for non-X—to say so would be a species of informal fallacy, akin to begging the question or an appeal to authority. The mere *pathos* of transformation cannot be used as a guarantor of its validity; so why even consider it? It is worthy of reflection because it may throw light on what it means to be transformed. What, then, might be a shared sentiment about our reality when we reflect on the five dialogic sketches of transformation, the fourth of which is that wrought by doing metaphysics? In all of the samples there seems to be a curious duality: on the one hand, the transformation in each case seems self-wrought; it is *my* fear that is transformed to courage by *my* confronting it. On the other, however, especially since it is presented in a dramatic form, it seems almost fated, as if the event or occasion were somehow designed, or at least waiting like a trap in the inevitable pathway. It is for this reason that each transformation in the sketches is evoked by a single word, suggesting that since we already know the word *loyalty* the mere mention of it in the sketch on the trial scene suffices to bring with it an entire reinterpretation of the evidence. So there is something of an enigma: transformation, though generated from within, seems to have a fatelike inevitability about it, as if I were inevitably made free to learn of my own inevitability. But this reflection seems to answer the question, What, if any, experiential phenomena may reflect metaphysical transformation? The last of the five sketches and all of chapter 6 reveals the answer: the phenomenon of learning. We know *palpably* what it is like to learn something; when what we learn is our own ability to think about being real, we become other than we were, as prisoners released from a cave. This release is a transformation.

Index